Inside a curriculum
project

M. D. Shipman
D. Bolam and D. R. Jenkins

Inside a curriculum project

A case study in the process
of curriculum change

Methuen & Co Ltd
11 New Fetter Lane   London EC4

First published 1974 by Methuen & Co Ltd
11 New Fetter Lane, London EC4P 4EE
© 1974 M. D. Shipman, D. Bolam and D. R. Jenkins
Printed in Great Britain by
Butler & Tanner Ltd, Frome and London

ISBN 0 416 78040 7 (hardback)
ISBN 0 416 78050 4 (paperback)

Distributed in the USA by
Harper & Row Publishers Inc,
Barnes & Noble Import Division

Contents

Contents

Preface

This book is a case study in curriculum change. It is first a description of the way one Schools Council curriculum project was established and implemented. Second, it is an investigation of the impact of this project on the trial schools that were involved and of the impact of those schools on the project. Third, it is an analysis of the influence exerted on curriculum change by the many agents involved in education. Finally, these aspects are viewed, not only from the researcher's angle, but from the inside of the project through chapters by the Project Director, David Bolam, and the Assistant Director, David Jenkins. In addition there are end-of-chapter comments by Jenkins and by Geoffrey Hartley and Alan Townsend, two of the project coordinators.

It is important to establish what was not covered by this investigation. First, there was no evaluation of integrated studies in the classroom. This was the concern of the project team. Second, it is not a contribution to the current debate over the suitability of the various theoretical models in curriculum theory. Third, while written by a sociologist, it was not planned to be an analysis of the spread of integrated studies at a time of rapid social change. The questions asked were about the way innovations are organized and spread. The answers may help in the planning of future development projects and in understanding the context in which such development has to be negotiated.

In many ways the Keele Integrated Studies Project was typical of the first phase of curriculum development projects financed by the Schools Council in the late 1960s. But integrated studies necessitated changes across a number of subject areas. It also involved new roles for teachers, especially in team teaching. It usually meant an increase in the amount of enquiry-based learning. It often led to mixed ability grouping. This combination of changes in school organization, particularly in timetabling, exceeded that in most other projects. Even more important, integration and the way it was implemented in trial schools imposed a greater strain on participating teachers for whom integrated studies were usually a new experience. In addition to these radical changes in the schools, the organization of the project was unusual in being designed to promote local initiatives rather than to dispense packaged ideas from the university. These differences mean that caution has to be exercised before generalizing. But this style of project design has become more popular in the 1970s and this increases the importance of the experience at Keele.

This was opportunistic research. I arrived at Keele as a curriculum project was being organized in an area of the curriculum in which I had been training teachers for the previous eight years. I had already been concerned with the development of humanities courses in one of the local authority areas that was involved. I had already carried out a small-scale investigation of the effects of introducing a curriculum innovation into secondary schools (Walton 1971). The project team was thinking of the contribution of sociology to curriculum packs and of finding consultants to help with evaluation. My request to study the development of the project and particularly its relations with schools was met with enthusiasm.

However, one obvious conclusion from the experience gained during this investigation, and one that recurs in this book, is, as Bolam has put it in Chapter 8, the impossibility of the outsider feeling what it was really like. Thus my interpretation of events observed differed from that of those actually engaged. One advantage of including comments from insiders is to highlight this difference, which is rarely examined in the reports of observational studies. Another is to show that the views of those on the inside also differ between themselves. Bolam, Jenkins and I give very different interpretations of the job definition and division of labour in the project team, of the part the teachers' centre was to play, of relations with publishers and, most important of all, of the definition of integration. The documents issued by the project gave a clear and consistent definition. Behind the scenes there was a continuing debate that made the observer's task fascinating.

It would also be misleading to suggest that the researcher's role was consistent. I was accepted as a sociologist who would observe, question and test. But I soon became participant observer, then took on small jobs for the team as participant without observing, and by the end seemed to have a consultant role on the professional side and was one of the boys on the personal side. This made it a delightful enterprise and enabled this blend of insider/outsider report to be produced. But it may have reduced my objectivity. Personally and professionally I think it was worth it, but the contributions of the project team members in this text are important checks on my interpretation.

To give some of the flavour of difference between outsider and insider, here are Jenkins's comments on the first draft of this Preface, in which I wrote that the project team had accepted an outside researcher in its midst for three years:

> Shipman does injustice to the complexity of his relationship with the course team. He began as wallpaper, making unthreatening non-noises, but soon his dormant position came under pressure from two directions. First the methodology of participant observation became a team in-joke, attracting banter ('Why is Shipman covering up his notes with his hand?'). Second, the team saw Shipman as a person well able to work his passage. Invitations to participate rather than observe were parried in crucial areas, but accepted in others. The knife-edge walked by this particular 'detached observer' is insufficiently acknowledged here. In general he tried to keep his counsel in meetings, but offer

support outside, e.g. with in-service training to encourage the social science contribution. The occasional doubt persisted ('Do you think Shipman *really* believes in what we're doing?').

There is one other gap in my outsider's view that is not necessarily plugged by the insiders. Particularly in the early planning days before the project team was appointed, there were meetings and telephone calls that were not documented. At the crucial point where the final form of the proposal was being negotiated there were meetings over lunch, at the National Liberal Club and in hotels that were only vaguely remembered by those attending but at which crucial decisions were made.

The inevitability of such gaps in the knowledge of the history of a project that lasted over four years makes the contributions by Bolam and Jenkins to this book so important. Everyone sees a different moving picture of an event in which all are involved. There are differences in interpretation and disagreement about what actually happened, but these are not necessarily right or wrong. The accounts differ because we all played a different part in the same ball game. The first five chapters are my view of the development of the project. Jenkins has appended footnotes commenting on this account. Bolam gives the Project Director's view in Chapter 8 and Jenkins analyses the responses of teachers in Chapter 6.

Many people were generous in giving time and information to me while realizing that all they would get back would be a critical published version of what they had said. Researchers are necessarily parasites. Yet everyone encouraged me as I probed. For three years the project team accepted a sociologist lurking in their midst, knowing that he was financed independently in case anything particularly nasty needed to be published. It was in this knowledge that the Schools Council and the Director of the Keele Institute of Education opened their books to me. No other curriculum project has been scrutinized in this intimate yet ruthless way. Yet alongside this investigation was an observers' panel of local authority advisers and college of education lecturers evaluating the project in the classrooms of the trial schools.

This book reflects therefore the generosity of all those involved who accepted me with such good grace. Particular thanks are due to Margaret Brooksbank, Geoffrey Hartley, Stanley Parker and Alan Townsend, the project team coordinators. David Bolam and David Jenkins, the Director and Assistant Director, have contributed to the book. They also had most to lose through the investigation. Thanks are also due to the officers of the Schools Council, the local authority advisers, the members of the observers' panel, the head-teachers and above all the teachers in the trial schools. Chapters 3 and 7 were developed out of articles published in the *Journal of Curriculum Studies* and Chapter 6 out of an article for the Open University. The diagrams by Bolam are reproduced by the generous consent of the Editor of *Ideas*, the curriculum magazine published by University of London, Goldsmiths' College. Finally I would like to thank the Nuffield Foundation for funding the research and the University of Keele for making it all possible.

Marten Shipman

1. Problems in establishing an innovation

Planned curriculum change is not new in English education. What is new is the urgency of such planning in the last two decades. The early focus was primarily on the reform of science teaching, but in the 1960s the humanities moved into the limelight. This concern arose partly out of the Newsom Report of 1963 where the need to reform the curriculum for the average and below average pupil in the secondary schools was stressed. Up to 1960 history and geography, taught as separate subjects, were usually considered sufficient by themselves. But in the next decade these subjects broadened in scope and social studies in some form began to appear in the secondary schools. Social studies had for long cut across subject boundaries in the primary schools and now the integration of previously subject-bound areas of knowledge received support in the secondary sector.

This move towards more social and integrated studies was reinforced by the drawn-out debate over the raising of the school leaving age. There was unanimity over the need for a new curriculum for the young school leaver once the leaving age was sixteen. If that curriculum was to be interesting and useful it would have to be relevant to the lives of the pupils outside the schools. This was the educational context in which the Schools Council Integrated Studies Project was designed.

2 Inside a curriculum project

The establishment of the Schools Council in 1964 was a symptom of the urgency of the need for change. By 1973 the Council had launched 123 research and development projects. Sixteen of these were in the humanities. Most of the curriculum projects have consisted of small teams, usually centred in universities, concentrating on the production and trial of new materials before spreading the new ideas through publishing, courses and conferences. Curriculum development was seen as a scattering of seed in the form of projects in hope that the ideas produced would germinate, grow and spread.

Much of the case study in this book revolves around the problems of reconciling the different perspectives of the Schools Council, university, local authority and trial school teachers. The compromises that resulted will exasperate those who yearn for rapid centrally directed change and those who support change through initiatives in individual schools. But these compromises must be interpreted in the context of the organization of English education, which is itself a compromise. There is a continually shifting balance between central and local government, teacher unions, professional associations, universities, examination boards, trade unions and employers. This balance of interests is built into the Schools Council. A majority of teachers are represented on each main committee and cost is shared between the central government and the local authorities. The governing council has representatives from thirty-five different interest groups.

This context for curriculum change at the local level consisted of diverse groups each pressing what seemed to those involved to be reasonable and legitimate views.[1] The Keele project could only be launched after these interests had been contacted, consulted and reconciled. Even after launching, the need to reconcile contrasting interests delayed getting the project under full steam. The effort involved left less time to determine objectives and procedures in advance. The end-product of the project was determined in the field, in contact with the schools, not on the drawing board. Early project documents were full of curriculum theory and principles of integration. But in the end it was what worked that survived.

Early negotiations

The history of the Keele project started in 1965 when a paper was sent from the Schools Council to teacher organizations, local authorities and universities proposing local and regional centres for curriculum development. It linked this development with in-service training and envisaged a cooperative effort by local education authorities, universities and colleges of education. Each of the thirty-five to forty-five centres would be linked to the Schools Council. This structure for curriculum development and support was devised by Morrell, probably the most influential figure in the early days of the Council. It was never organized and Morrell did not stay long enough at the Council to push his ideas. Only the North West Regional Curriculum Development Project seems to have a direct link to the proposal. But the idea was accepted at Keele where steps were taken immediately to mobilize support for a regional centre.

The first step was to call a meeting and interest local authorities and colleges of education in the vicinity of the university. In May 1966 a committee was constituted under the title of the Keele Consultative Committee for Schools Council Proposals. Representatives came from colleges of education, the local authorities, the teachers, the inspectorate, the university and, later, the Schools Council. From records of early meetings there was some confusion about the meaning of the proposal from the Schools Council, but little opposition to the view of the university that a positive response should be made. The humanities and the school leaving programme were chosen as topics for concrete proposals to the Council and the university Institute of Education was asked to prepare drafts.

The first draft was presented to the committee in October 1966 and after many amendments the proposal for a project in the humanities was sent to the Schools Council in February 1967. These early negotiations not only determined the terms of reference for the Integrated Studies Project once it got down to work, but inadvertently placed it in a politically difficult position. The committee had discussed the school leaving age and humanities programmes as separate issues, but when the latter was prepared, many seemed to have assumed that the humanities proposal included that for a school leaving programme. The local authority advisers certainly claimed in interviews at the end of the project that this was their understanding. Thus the move towards working on integrated studies across the whole secondary school curriculum was seen by them as a double-double-cross. It deflected attention away from the problem of the young school leaver that was their major concern at this time and it seemed to lower the priority given to the humanities that were crucial for a relevant programme for the fifteen and sixteen year olds. This feeling of betrayal was confirmed when junior packs were prepared by the project team and packs for seniors in the secondary schools were left incomplete by the end of the trial.

This difference of interest also stopped any progress towards establishing any centre for general curriculum development at Keele. The humanities proposal was to be the only one ever presented. This was mainly due to the difficulty in reconciling the different interests brought to the committee. It was also due to the rapid turnover of key staff in the early days of the Schools Council and at the university.

The draft proposal

The proposals from Keele were finally accepted by the Schools Council in April 1967. There had been feverish activity over a couple of months as the usual economy cuts forced the Council to prune budgets. This curriculum project, and probably all the rest conceived at his time, was the product of frantic to-ing and fro-ing, of telephone messages interpreted in contrasting ways by those on each end of the line, of last-minute revisions to drafts that had taken months to prepare. There was no experience in designing curriculum projects. Large numbers were being considered and tidied up by only a few Schools Council officers, all of whom were new to the job. Looking at the correspondence, at the final draft proposals and at Schools Council committee papers of this period, brought home the remarkable achievement of getting so much off the ground in so short a time. Obviously mistakes were made and the overall strategy may have been suspect, but between 1964 and 1969 new network of projects was organized.

The final approved draft contained a unique staffing proposal. There was to be a full-time Director and an Assistant Director, but these would be supported by three or more full-time coordinators. These coordinators would be serving teachers whose work was known to be original and who would be seconded by their LEA for the duration of the project. The Director and Assistant Director were to be at Keele, but the coordinators would be based at points throughout the area in accommodation provided by the LEAs. In retrospect, this organization made the Keele Integrated Studies Project a case study in cooperation between a university-based project team and local authorities. It increased the sensitivity of the project to local needs and gave it a grassroots flavour. There were great advantages in this organization. However, the divided responsibility of the coordinators assumed a harmony between the project and local authorities that was sometimes difficult to sustain.

While the organization of the project was clearly laid down in the proposal, the terms of reference were left vague. Early drafts had just referred to a project on the humanities. The final proposal described it as part of a school leaving age project. An important aim was seen to be the investigation of possible means of integration within the humanities. After acceptance the project was referred to as concerned with the integration of the humanities, or, in some papers, the coordination of the humanities. In May 1967 it was being referred to as the Schools Council Study of the Coordination and Integration of the Humanities in Secondary Schools. In June it was referred to as the Keele Humanities Project.

These different titles reflected a fundamental difficulty in deciding the scope of this project. There were two possible interpretations.

One placed the emphasis on the humanities and was concerned with the subjects that could be included under this umbrella. The second was concerned with the possibilities and principles of integration.[2] Some idea of the difficulties in using this term can be gauged from the way the terms 'coordination' and 'integration' were used interchangeably in this early period. These two possibilities were further confused by the emphasis on the project being part of the school leaving age programme. Once the raising of the school leaving age was postponed, the need to consider this as a priority disappeared.

By the time the project team was appointed the humanities and their integration was the problem to be considered, across the whole of secondary schooling. The project team was to face a situation without clear guidelines. The only developed model for curriculum development was Nuffield Science, and most contemporary projects were starting under the Schools Council for the first time. There was also very little experience of humanities teaching in this country in the mid 1960s. This situation was probably shared by most of these first phase projects. The extreme alternatives were to go for a small, easily defined area of work and prepare a detailed set of proposals and curriculum materials, or to gather up information about existing work in schools and then present possibilities for a new curriculum. These questions would have to be answered by project teams who themselves had no experience of curriculum development. These early pioneers were having to carve out their own methods of working in a situation where, for the first time, a major national initiative was being taken to undertake innovation at local level.

The actual guideline for the project team within the original proposal read as follows:

> One of the principal purposes of this enquiry would be to explore possible *means* and *meaning* of *integration* in the humanities.
>
> The investigators will have to try to answer questions such as the following, providing data from the schools in this area:
>
> (i) How far does the organization of teaching in secondary

schools lead to a division of labour which runs counter to common strategy by the teachers?

(ii) What are the kinds of strategy employed in the humanities by teachers leading to the coordinated presentation of the subjects?

(iii) Is any attempt being made to see what kind of coordinated understanding pupils have of the humanities?

(iv) Is it possible to regroup ideas and knowledge between subjects in the humanities in the secondary school so as to provide new and intellectually reputable curricula?

(v) Are the 'expressive subjects' related to, can they be, or ought they to be related to the 'intellectual disciplines' in the humanities like English, history, languages?

(vi) In what sense if any is integration in the humanities taking place? Are there additional ways in which it should be attempted?

Answers to questions like these will be different for pupils of different ages and probably also for pupils of different ability levels.

Across the three years of the project this original proposal was to become increasingly remote from the actual work that was done.[3] The rest of this book is an account of the pressures that led to this transition. It is not a criticism of the original drafters of the proposals, but more a commentary on the process of innovation in education.

The Keele project probably suffered more than most from the difficulty of defining the area for research and development work. But it was typical of planned curriculum change in its exposure to the pressures of national and local interests, each of which was pressing its own case and trying to influence the project. Even the most precisely defined curriculum projects were exposed to these pressures. During the early negotiations the pressures were represented on the committees at local and national levels. Any product of two sets of committees is liable to lack sufficient definition. But this committee structure is a reflection of interests that will be at work on all projects. A balance has to be struck somewhere between entering the field with a clearly defined brief, which may then be rejected or frustrated by local interests, or entering with more flexible, if vague ideas which can be adjusted as the project develops. We know too little about the actual process of innovation in education to be confident that one method is superior to the other. There is probably room for both.

The research on which this book was based was not concerned with the evaluation of the curriculum materials and methods introduced into the trial schools. However, the relation between project team and schools which was of prime concern can be understood only in the light of developments recommended by the Integrated Studies Project. The publicity handout issued by the project in 1970 contained the following crucial points:

> RANGE OF ENQUIRY: The project is examining the problems and possibilities of integrated humanities courses, during the four years of secondary education (11–15) and across the whole ability range. The project is concerned centrally with the organization of learning most likely to lead to a relatedness of the disciplines and their distinct methods of enquiry and verification.
>
> 'HUMANITIES' & 'INTEGRATION': 'Humanities' are understood as any subject, or aspect of a subject, which contributes to the rational or imaginative understanding of the human situation. 'Integration' is understood as the exploration of any large area, theme or problem which:
>
> (a) requires the help of more than one subject discipline for its full understanding, and
>
> (b) is best taught by the concerted action of a group of teachers.

The direction of the changes proposed by the project for the role of the trial school teachers was as follows:

Traditional role	Proposed role
1. Subject based	1. Subjects integrated

2. Teaching by instruction   2. Fostering enquiry
3. Teaching individually   3. Team teaching

The changes proposed in the role of the teacher outlined above were not the result of a pattern imposed by the project on trial schools.[4] Nor did the team produce a full course. Curriculum units were produced with a request for a flexible, unstructured approach to the introduction of integrated studies. The new role was proposed but not imposed. The schools added another innovation themselves. In most cases the innovation was used as an opportunity for using unstreamed groups in schools where streaming was normal. This probably indicated a willingness to innovate as this project arrived.

The schools that joined in the project committed themselves to changes in organization that would facilitate the introduction of integrated studies. The major commitments were:

1. To plan the timetable to facilitate team teaching and enquiry methods.
2. To form teams of teachers willing to innovate.
3. To provide the resources that would enable children to learn actively through individual or group work.
4. To take an active part in feeding back ideas to the project team based at Keele.

These commitments meant that the schools were going to change the organization of a number of subjects. The innovation could not therefore be isolated within a school. It was a test of the ability of staff to change the curriculum across a substantial part of the total work of the school. Single subject curriculum projects do not face this difficulty. Furthermore, integrated studies is not an accepted subject like history or geography. The Keele project was more radical in its demands than other projects because of this focus on an untried area of work which would cut across existing curriculum arrangements.

10   Inside a curriculum project

Thirty-eight schools were involved in the project between 1968 and 1971. They were composed as follows:

Trial period

1969–1970	1970–1971
3 Grammar schools*	2 Grammar schools
3 Comprehensive schools	4 Comprehensive schools
22 Modern schools	19 Modern schools
5 Junior high schools†	2 Junior high schools
	1 Middle school (9–13 years)

* One of these grammar schools became a comprehensive school within this period.

† These schools were starting to become comprehensive during this period.

Some 220 teachers were involved with the project, an average of six per school. All were engaged in some subject teaching as well as integrated studies through some form of team teaching.

There were four categories of school:

1. 22 schools that worked within the project in 1969–70 and again in 1970–1.
2. 4 schools that worked within the project in 1969–70 but then continued with their own version of Integrated Studies in 1970–1.
3. 7 schools that worked within the project in 1969–70 but dropped out at the end of the year 1970 or failed to complete their trial work in 1970–1.
4. 5 schools that joined the project for work in 1970–71.

The trial schools ranged in size from a two-form entry secondary modern school to a nine-form entry comprehensive school. They were chosen to represent rural, urban and suburban areas. But there were two features that stopped the trial school sample being representative:

(1) There were only eight of the thirty-seven secondary schools where third forms were included in the trial. Two of these eight dropped out within a year and two more were among the four schools that left in the first year to develop their own version of integrated studies. Thus only four schools having a full trial included third forms. The reason given by teachers was that this was the year in which subject choices were made for future work in senior forms. A division into separate subjects was seen as necessary in third forms to ensure that there had been the experience on which such choices could be made. First and second forms could be given integrated studies. It was popular for fourth forms not taking external examinations. But third forms were seen as the start of the various paths into top streams and integration would have provided no basis for choice.

(2) Schools were reluctant to involve senior examination forms in integrated studies. Trial was limited to forms that would not be taking external examinations or that took integrated studies as a substitute for general studies. This was being overcome by the end of the trial period once CSE Integrated Studies Mode 3 schemes had been negotiated. But these negotiations were complicated by the need to ensure that integrated studies would count for more than a single pass, having replaced a number of individual subjects each counting as a pass.

There was a great variety in the commitments of schools to the trial. None accepted the Schools Council view that their main responsibility was to the trial. All saw the conditions for joining as secondary to the ongoing work of the school. The teachers thought they were doing the project team a favour. In five schools teachers even claimed that they were not really part of the trial but were just helping out.[5]

Underlying this reluctance of teachers and heads to accept the priority of ensuring a genuine trial situation was an unresolved tension. The request to experiment and the absence of a clear blueprint should have encouraged innovations tailored to the conditions in individual schools. Yet the teachers simultaneously asked for a packaged deal that would relieve them of the need to work out strategies for themselves. The teachers seemed to demand both a detailed plan for action and freedom to adjust to local school contexts. They asked to be told what to do, only to reject the suggestions as unsuitable for their school. Much of the analysis that follows is concerned with the view from the classroom that seems to lie at the core of this contradiction.

◆◆ Comments by D. R. Jenkins

[1] An interesting perspective. But this 'conflict model' would be misleading if it were taken to imply that there was some kind of free-for-all. A rhetoric of legitimation already existed, organized around the notion that the Schools Council and its curriculum projects exist to 'extend the range of choice available to teachers'. Although there are ambiguities (like maintaining concurrently that the curriculum is a legitimate object of social policy), projects themselves have some difficulty in claiming 'interests' beyond the interests of the schools they serve. They need to articulate problems all right, but we still need to ask the question 'Whose problems?' A curriculum project can probably make demands during the trial period by pleading a research paradigm ('What the trial school owes the project') but the Keele Integrated Studies Project tended to underbid on this part of its hand.

[2] Since the 'two possible interpretations' put forward are not logically distinct, still less mutually exclusive, it is difficult to feel that they represented a real choice. It may be that antecedent documents display a nervousness or uncertainty in this area, but I cannot

recall a time when the project's grappling with the principles of integration did not subsume epistemological questions and a consideration of school subjects. The project's brief was to examine a number of questions. Two of the most important were in the guidelines:

1. How far does the organization of teaching in secondary schools lead to a division of labour which runs counter to the production of a common strategy by teachers?
2. Is it possible to regroup ideas and knowledge between subjects in the humanities in secondary school so as to provide new and intellectually reputable data?

A later definition was to my view more confusing. At one point integration was defined as 'the exploration of any large area, theme or problem which (*a*) requires the help of more than one subject or discipline for its full understanding, and (*b*) is best taught by the concerted action of a group of teachers'. The second assertion seems to be a recommendation rather than a definition of integration, but needs to be seen in the context of Bolam's view that definitions 'serve as a focus in negotiations with teachers'. Certainly the project went overboard for a team teaching model. In retrospect I am not too sure why alternatives were not built in, since the connection is at best contingent rather than logical.

[3] This was mainly because the project accepted the conventional wisdom of trial, that the production of novel curriculum material should back up the ideas being explored. Questions about the rationale of a project involve an implicit appeal to consider its internal logic. Not all the questions can be reinterpreted as questions about how to develop curriculum material. Nor is it too clear how the questions posed by the guidelines could be empirically tested during trial. One way of partly resolving these differences would be to say that the project was both articulating a new tradition and giving examples of representative work within it. This means that

the guidelines were taken as indicating issues rather than as suggesting research hypotheses.

[4] Yes, of course. The project became caught up in a number of fashionable stances not logically connected with its task. A move towards learning by enquiry is neutrally related both to team teaching and to the integration of subjects. This is not to say that one possible model of integration could not begin with a view of enquiry (as does IDE as proposed by the Goldsmiths Curriculum Laboratory). Enquiry is more often associated in curriculum theory with the models of enquiry of contributing disciplines. In general, however, the trial schools were less interested in inducting pupils into established modes of enquiry and more interested in pursuing a loose child-centredness.

[5] This certainly rings true. I am reminded of Albert Reiss's 'The social integration of queers and peers' (1968). Homosexual prostitutes did not necessarily define themselves as queer. It was not their needs being satisfied. They too were 'just helping out'. When Shipman talks about a 'genuine trial situation' and the school's inability to accept its claims, he is being over-generous to the project. We never resolved this one ourselves. First and foremost the 'unresolved tension' was inside the project. The demands made were unclear, and when clear were not insisted on, as evidenced in the shambles over teacher (as opposed to coordinator) feedback.

2. Communication and identification

As soon as the Schools Council approved the proposal for a project in the integration of the humanities, the Keele Consultative Committee assumed that it would appoint a Director and Assistant Director. The organization of the project would be guided by an advisory committee drawn from Keele, the local colleges of education, the local education authorities and the teachers. Each local authority involved would second one teacher to serve as coordinator within the project team. In practice, however, these arrangements proved very difficult to implement because of the diverse interests that had to be reconciled.

Establishing an advisory committee

The first difficulty in communication arose between the Schools Council and the Keele Consultative Committee. The Council wanted a small contact committee to ensure liaison between them and the project as it developed. They also wanted a larger steering committee, which would not, at least at first, be concerned with detail. It was to be representative of local and national interests and would become a full consultative committee when the project was ready to make crucial decisions over the production for publication of curriculum materials. Significantly this was the first mention of publication, which had not appeared in the original proposal. The Schools Council seems to have assumed that this was the way projects would develop. By the time the project team was appointed this view seems to have prevailed at Keele as well. Those appointed were given the impression that the sequence of events would be an examination of feasibility, then trial and publication.

The Schools Council's reference to a small contact committee was not expected at Keele. The impression of the Director of the Institute of Education at Keele who had been responsible for the early negotiations was that Schools Council representation on the Keele Consultative Committee would suffice. The Schools Council, however, assuming from this early stage that curriculum materials would be published, saw the need for a bigger committee with representatives of national interests so that support could be mobilized at the time when ideas and materials were ready for distribution. There would therefore be a need for a smaller, more specialized and local committee to guide the project in the early stages. It was finally agreed that the single advisory committee proposed by Keele would be established and that consideration of broadening its membership be left for the time being. The final shape of this committee can be seen in Figure 1 produced by Bolam (1973), the Project Director.

The Schools Council also favoured more teacher representation on the advisory committee than was originally proposed at Keele. However, these additional appointments proved difficult to make. There was a long gap between nominations being requested and names arriving. From November 1967 to January 1968 letters flowed between Keele and the local education authorities over the number of teachers that should serve and over the way they should be nominated. Each authority seemed to want a different number. But the solution to the numbers to be appointed coincided with a new diplomatic incident as the teacher unions objected to the approach being made through the local authorities. This turned out to be a pointless argument. Having established their right to

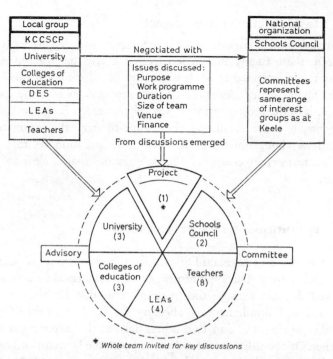

Figure 1 *The setting up of the advisory committee*

1. The initiative started with the Keele Consultative Committee for Schools Council Projects (KCCSCP). It was intended that this should represent all the key educational interests within the area, so that any project should have their full backing.

2. Negotiations were undertaken with the Schools Council, who needed to be satisfied that the proposal had effective support and was viable. In this context 'Schools Council' means its key secretaries and committees, who make the basic decisions involving policy and finance. Thus a different group of people were involved than those with whom the project was to have a close working relationship. The decision machinery, so to speak, of the Council was not used again until the project requested an extension of time.

3. Throughout its life the project was guided by an advisory committee, whose membership reflected the range of all the interests who had been involved in the original negotiations. The only exception was the DES, but the local HMI continued as a member of the KCCSCP, of which the advisory committee was constitutionally a subcommittee. The figures in the segments of the circle, showing the advisory committee, are the number of people involved.

increased representation, the teachers never attended in force.[1] Indeed, those finally nominated from the area that caused most delay rarely attended at all. It took until March 1968 for this issue to be finally settled. As in the original negotiations over the establishment of the project, priority was given to reconciling conflicting interests in order to obtain the means to start the innovation. Decisions about objectives received little attention so that the project team received more a list of questions than a clear assignment.

The appointment of a project team

The Director and Assistant Director for the project were appointed in October 1967. The appointment of local teachers as coordinators proved difficult because the financial crisis that hit the Schools Council was simultaneously affecting the local authorities. Two decided not to join and two others delayed the secondment of a teacher. One coordinator was appointed with the Director and Assistant Director and started work with them in January 1968. Another started part-time on this date. It was only in September 1968 that all four coordinators were appointed and by this time the first appointed had resigned and been replaced. This staggered appointment not only delayed the collection of information from the schools on current teaching in the humanities, but increased the problem of establishing a project identity that could unite the team and project a public image. At Schools Council, on the advisory committee and on the project team there was turnover of crucial personnel at an early stage. At the same time there was a change of Director of the Institute of Education at Keele.

This difficulty over identity arose partly out of the extensive terms of reference given to the project team. Priority had to be given to deciding where the emphasis was to be placed, whether on problems of integration or on the development of materials for teaching in the humanities. Those appointed had first to define the objectives of the project, then to define the way they would work. They were not appointed to do a clearly defined job. They had first to work out what the intentions of those who established the project really were.

The collection of information on work in the humanities reduced the need to determine where the emphasis of the project would lie. Two distinct lines of development soon became visible. First, there was the attempt to define what was meant by the integration of the humanities. Second there was the attempt, particularly from the coordinators, to focus attention on the actual work that was being done in the local schools and the possibilities for developing new approaches in them.[2] The reconciliation of the academic and the pragmatic view came through the decision to concentrate attention on the production of curriculum materials for the schools. These materials would be designed to facilitate integration across subject boundaries, but would leave schools with the decision about which subjects to integrate. By March 1968 the first suggestions for curriculum packs were given titles.[3] By September 1968 the titles of five packs, all concerned with social life, had been approved by the advisory committee. From February 1969 these packs were developed with a view to eventual publication. Once the trial of these packs in schools started in September 1969 there were regular meetings with the proposed publisher. The final form of these units is described in the extract from a project information sheet that follows:

TEACHING MATERIAL & APPROACHES:

(a) *General:*
The project is not producing a full course. Instead, it is developing a number of curriculum units to exemplify different patterns of integration. For this purpose, 'humanities' is interpreted widely enough to include elements of the natural sciences and technology, and stresses the complementary importance of the arts and the social sciences. The

units are focused on themes of basic human importance which may not be, or are only in part, controversial. The units are aimed at different age groups, and have a general emphasis on the learning of skills and large explaining concepts.[4] The approach involves some form of team teaching, and is based on the conviction that integrated units are viable within a number of organizational patterns.

(b) *Curriculum units:*

Each unit contains an analysis of the area of enquiry, suggested activity patterns, teaching materials, and information on further sources.

The selected themes are:

For Juniors (Forms 1 and 2):

  (i) *Exploration Man* – an introductory pack which explores the meaning of being human.

  (ii) *Communication* – basic skills and approaches of the creative arts.

  (iii) *Living Together* – same, for social sciences.

For Middle School (Forms 3 and 4):

  (i) *Development in West Africa* – a regional study.

  (ii) *Man-Made Man* – both the 'image of man' in creative arts, as well as the extension of man's capacities through technology.

  (iii) *Groups in Society* – the problem of groups in conflict with majority opinion.

None of the project team had had previous experience of research and development work.[5] The division of labour, the way of working and the content of the curriculum materials produced reflect the different interests of the members of project team. This personal element in curriculum development cannot be overlooked. No given terms of reference could exclude them. In the Keele project, where the terms of reference were only broadly defined, the scope for individual determination of the outcomes was great. Some curriculum projects seem to reflect the views of the project director. Others reflect the nature of the subject under development. But it is in the interaction between the project team and the schools using the curriculum materials that the personal contribution of any team member can be developed. The schools actively interpret communications from projects. They extract and emphasize those elements that suit their local needs. But this emphasis within trial schools reinforces the hand of the project team member responsible for initiating a particular component. One school would be keen on studying Gypsies. Another would be enthusiastic about life in the North American frontier towns as settlers moved west. Another would seize upon the idea of a resource centre as the crucial element in the development of humanities teaching. Another would go overboard on team teaching. Any project team sensitive to communication from the schools comes under conflicting pressures. Individual members of the team can always find reinforcement for their own views.

The university as project base

The original proposals for the Integrated Studies project were made by the Director of the Institute of Education at Keele and the project headquarters was housed in the university. This had many advantages. It provided a central base not under the control of any one local authority. Through the Area Training Organization there were existing links with local colleges of education which were to prove receptive to the idea of integration. Above all it gave the project the prestige of Keele and this label was to prove useful to trial school teachers, as they experimented in their schools.

There were disadvantages, however. The project team got heavily involved in in-service courses within the Institute of Education.[6] It was also committed to helping the colleges of education to establish integrated courses. But the biggest disadvantage came from the same source as the main strength. The prestige of a university is

B

associated with academic work that is seen by teachers as far removed from their battleground in the classroom. Keele was a support used by teachers in the trial for defending integrated studies against criticism from colleagues in the schools, but the university was simultaneously associated with the theoretical, detached academic approach which contrasted starkly with the pragmatic, concrete interests of front-line teachers.

There was an accompanying ambivalence in the attitudes of teachers towards the project directors at Keele. Many took the view from the trenches, scorning the impractical, unreal communiqués from headquarters well behind the front. These teachers found it self-evident that those directing the project had never taught in schools. But a few seemed to yearn for contact with academics who could provide ideas and intellectual rigour. There were even teachers who held both views simultaneously. One enterprising yet critical teacher who had extracted a lot from the project expressed it this way when interviewed after the end of the trial:

> It was cheek, really. All we got was drivel about logical development. We knew they were not really teachers but they should have stopped telling us how to do our jobs. What I wanted was, I don't know, inspiration, something to tell me what I was supposed to be doing. I've been to a university and I expected to be treated as part of it again. We got a royal visit and a few kind words after we joined but nothing we could get our teeth into.

The impression obtained in the interviews with teachers was that the ablest and most lively were eager to embrace their academic suitors and join in the debate about the direction in which integration would take education. But they withdrew because all they could offer was the folk wisdom of the classroom. In reality it was this exchange of central knowledge and local experience that was the rationale behind the organization of the project. The appointed members of the project team were all from teaching and had them-

selves to accommodate to working in a university. They were committed to working with trial school teachers to collect information
and develop new ideas and materials. The organization shown in
Figure 2 was built round a teachers' centre. This was where the
exchange of views would take place and where the real curriculum
development would take place.

Figure 2 *Proposed project organization 1968*

Negotiations with the Schools Council over the teachers' centre
started in December 1967. The centre was described in the application for extra funds as vital for the success of the project. The
Schools Council was encouraging and said that a small supplementary sum might be available, but insisted that the money for it
should come from the funds allocated for the project, with the local
authorities contributing for services offered that were not related to
the project.

In February 1968 a request was made to the Schools Council for
funds to set up the centre and for running expenses for the three
years of the life of the project. The Director of the Keele Institute
of Education had written to the Schools Council making it clear
that 'the establishment of a teachers' centre will be vital to the success of the project'.[7] The centre was to provide:

1 A forum for the discussion of ideas and the production of
  materials.
2 A full context. The range of the centre's concern would enable
  the project to see its research in the widest possible setting,

showing where it can work in secondary schools related to similar exploration in the primary school at the one end and in colleges of further education at the other.

3 Continuity. The centre's organization would be the appropriate body for following up the work at the completion of the project.

The centre was also recommended to the Schools Council as a means of coordinating regional participation in the project. But in July 1968 the Schools Council decided that the centre must be financed out of funds already allocated to the project and that an application for extra money should be made later when expenses could be calculated more accurately.

From this point the proposals for a teachers' centre were scaled down to a resource centre. This amended proposal avoided duplication with local authority plans for curriculum development centres. The authorities had already decided not to give financial support to a centre at Keele. The new resource centre was to offer:

1 A resource bank.
2 The opportunity for any trial school teacher to be on limited secondment (perhaps two weeks would be an average) to the team, to share thinking and prepare resources or material. Technical help would be available.

This resource centre was to be open before the start of the trial in the schools in September 1969. In practice the teachers rarely used the centre and by the start of the trial it was more a storage than a workshop centre.[8] It never formed an important part of the communication network within which it was originally seen as the hub. A decentralized project was still a possibility but now depended on the teachers in the schools developing their own versions within the framework of ideas provided from Keele. As long as this local initiative went on and the products were fed back to Keele for distribution to other schools and for incorporation into project materials centralization could be avoided. The difficulties experienced by the teachers in fulfilling this commitment are dealt with in Chapter 5. The difference between the proposed and actual organization of the project which resulted from the absence of an active teachers' centre can be seen in Figure 2 on p. 23 and Figure 4 on p. 65.

Mobilizing the trial schools

There was no simple sequence of events through which a school joined the trial. The variety of procedures was as great as the differing commitments of the schools once they were in. The most usual sequence was for the approach to the local authority to be followed by a meeting called to explain the project to those interested. This was usually attended by heads. In some areas this was followed by a meeting with advisory staff to decide which schools would be suitable for a trial. There would then be visits to the schools to give further details, meet the staff and obtain cooperation.

However, there were wide differences between local authority areas. At one extreme the local advisory staff took a very active part in the selection of schools. But in another they seemed to have left the choice of schools to the project team. After the finish of the trial some advisers could not remember how or why schools in their area had been selected.[9] Even more remarkable, teachers and heads found it difficult to remember how they became a trial school. Teachers in five trial schools were even convinced that they had never really joined. In the interviews after the end of the trial they maintained that they were only obliging the team by trying out a particular curriculum unit but had not accepted any obligations.[10] In two of these schools the bewilderment at being treated as part of the trial was probably justified as the project team only recognized thirty-six not thirty-eight as the number really involved.

These variations in the way schools became involved and the different levels of commitment partly account for the different impact of the project in the schools. But there was another important factor outside the schools at this early stage. Some local authorities gave trial schools extra cash, but others insisted that extra costs should be borne out of existing funds. In one area the library service rallied to support trial schools. But there was no support that could be anticipated or expected. The context of innovation seemed to have been determined by chance not design.

The project and the schools

The first months of the project's work consisted of visits to schools to find out the extent of integrated studies teaching.[11] Once it was decided that a number of trial schools should be selected to try out new curriculum materials from September 1969 the purpose of visits became more the selection of promising schools until the thirty required had been collected. During 1968 and early 1969 the project team was trying to inform schools of the objectives of the project and trying to interest teachers in integrated studies. This not only involved visits to schools and talks to teachers' groups, but conferences held at Keele. But at these conferences, and in the various circulars sent to interested schools by the project team, there was a serious communication gap. Questions from the floor consisted largely of complaints about jargon and lack of concrete advice about how to work with poor readers or the third-form Mafia. Curriculum theory is a relatively new area of study. It has rapidly developed a language of its own. But this is not the 'language' used by teachers. The attempt to interest the teachers in principles of integration and various theories of the curriculum failed. Teachers, supported by local authority advisers, responded with vigour and scorn.[12] Here are a selection of comments from interviews:

> There were too many meetings and handouts early on. I gave up going to Keele and threw the papers away. I'd better things to do than read that rubbish.

We didn't need ideas but contact with lively minds in person. What we got was a jargon-loaded diatribe that alienated many people. It emphasized how out of touch research and teaching is nowadays.

There was a complete misunderstanding of the level at which teachers are prepared to be interested. They weren't on a course in curriculum theory, they were doing their best to keep afloat in classrooms.

The language of early documents was unnecessarily complicated. In team meetings the coordinators were also critical of early documentation. Alan Townsend, a coordinator, commenting on this text, saw it this way:

As someone joining the team two terms after the start of the project and perhaps feeling somewhat threatened by the level of theoretical discussion and the specialized vocabulary through which it was being expressed, there was some reluctance on my part to question as rigorously as I should have done, and later did, the language and texture of some of the documents directed at teachers and particularly those documents designed for fairly wide general distribution. Only at the end of the first term in the team was I sufficiently relaxed and sure of myself in my new role to be more questioning and forceful in this matter. This problem of the language level in documents for outside consumption was never really solved (even if it could have been), and not even admitted to by one member of the team. The assumption was wrongly made that the teachers in general were reading widely in the theory and current practice in their own subject.

The level of abstraction in documents was not simply a matter of jargon. The members of the project team felt that they had a responsibility to put basic issues before teachers to ensure that the implications of introducing integrated studies were understood.

They realized that integration was a complicated process and that there was a danger that teachers would join the trial with enthusiasm but without sufficient realization of the snags. Even worse, there was the likelihood that curriculum materials published after the trial would be used without any attention being paid to the principles that accounted for their format and for recommended learning strategies.

Many teachers only realized the importance of the theoretical discussion of integration after they had experienced the practical difficulties of implementing integrated studies in their schools. Thus most teachers had thrown away the documents from the team before they came to realize their importance. Again and again in this study the same sequence occurred. The team had to explain what it was going to do before it could do it. The teachers started by doing it and only then looked for an explanation of why they were doing it that way. In the interviews after the trial had ended there were teachers who criticized the absence of information on principles and problems of integration. Two years before these same teachers were vocal in complaining that all they got from Keele were abstract long-winded and complicated theoretical papers.

In the schools teachers seemed reconciled to this difficulty, seeming to expect it. One teacher summed up the problem by criticizing the jargon at meetings and in documents, but accepting that there was blame on both sides, and tersely wrote 'Lacking! Both ways' on a questionnaire as a description of communications between school and Keele after paying tribute to the efforts made by the team to keep in touch. Here was another symptom of the tendency of teachers to want both academic rigour and easy-bake recipes from the same source.

In this communication gap lies the source of the difficulty in getting teachers to feed back information to a project. This difficulty is partly a consequence of the extra work that was involved, but it was also the consequence of a rejection by the teachers of the value of the sort of information that was being requested by the team.[13]

Teachers are forced to be pragmatists. As long as something pro-
mised to work they would try it. They were not, however, willing
to engage in a debate over issues that did not seem to help them face
the problems of the classroom. The Keele project had a great
advantage in the employment of coordinators linking the schools
with the project. These coordinators were critical of the obscurity
of documents at project team meetings, and, with one foot in the
pragmatic and the other in the academic camp, could bring back the
necessary information themselves. Within two months of the start
of the trial period in September 1969 they had detected the schools
that were not genuinely implementing the project. They were
sympathetic to the views of the teachers yet could see the need for
a more theoretical approach by the project. As a consequence the
communication gap did not prove too much of an obstacle.
Furthermore, this was a very local project covering a small geo-
graphical area. Throughout this early period the project team were
well aware of the communication problems. In the first two terms
of trial the team tried unsuccessfully to design schedules that would
be filled in and returned by teachers.[14] Looking back, it was as if
the project was operating at two levels. On one level the work had
to stand up to academic criticism. Simultaneously the project was
operating at a much more practical level helping teachers in the
classroom to develop suitable material and methods of working.
Projects with a national coverage would have more difficulty
reconciling these contrasting approaches.

There was one important, yet unanticipated, spin-off from the
local nature of this project. This was the development of local, lateral
communications between the schools. Sometimes this occurred
through meetings organized by the project at Keele. The teachers
who were interviewed were unanimous in the view that the benefits of those conferences came, not from the speakers, but from the
opportunity to discuss ongoing work with teachers in other schools.
There were also meetings in the teachers' centres developed in one
local authority area which served the same purpose. Often these
were workshop sessions deliberately organized by the coordinators

to enable teachers to exchange ideas. Others were to acquaint teachers with views on the themes by social scientists. But even where there was a team member or expert to introduce the session, the teachers welcomed most the chance to see what their neighbours were doing. It was very noticeable that in the local authority that had established teachers' centres there was more of this lateral communication and exchange of ideas than in those areas where the development of teachers' centres had been delayed. In retrospect this underlines the disadvantages of not establishing a teachers' centre specifically to develop the ideas of the teachers involved in the project at Keele. Yet this may have been geographically too distant for many of the schools.

The distances were not great in this project. Few schools were over fifty miles away from Keele. Yet after a day's work in school there was little incentive to travel this distance to attend a conference. It is a tribute to the teachers and to their headteachers that the attendance of the more distant schools was as good or even better than schools neighbouring Keele. The interviews showed that the reason for this was the feeling in rural schools that they needed to find out what was going on elsewhere. Teachers were asked, at the end of the project, which schools they had been in contact with during the two trial years. Schools in heavily built-up areas tended to have little contact with other schools that had introduced integrated studies. But there were interesting local networks in the rural areas. These consisted either of two or three schools around the same small town, or schools in small towns stretched along a linking major road. It must be stressed that the establishment of these informal communication links was voluntary. The teachers involved had given up their spare time to travel to other schools to find out what was going on. One local authority had encouraged this by holding local meetings at which the teachers could exchange ideas. These meetings were held to exchange ideas about the teaching of humanities generally; but the Keele project was asked to play a prominent part. But this cooperation was still mixed with misunderstandings about motives. Some meetings organized by local authority advisers were seen by the project team not to be aimed at spreading the idea of integration, but at undermining it and replacing work sponsored by the Keele project with other work supported by the advisers.

The organization of this rival scheme for integrated studies was queried during an interview with the adviser responsible. He expressed surprise that it should have been taken as a hostile act. He admitted that he had not thought about the effect on the project, but explained this as follows:

> We have some fifty secondary schools in this county. Five were in the Keele project. I suppose it seemed a big thing to the Keele team but it was just a small part of my total plan. Anyway our interest in humanities came before the Schools Council came on the scene. It will be there when the project has ended. I don't see that there was any confusion in the schools and, after all, we found the schools for them.

At this point his colleague added:

> You rush around in this job and there are so many projects in the schools that you can't stop every time you meet one. To be honest I think we were doing a better job. We should have done as we knew the schools so well. I like a lot of the materials. We will use it when it's ready. But at the start there was a lot that could not be used.

It will be argued later that this was not just a breakdown in communication, although advisers were on the advisory committee of the project. It was rather the difficulty of approaching the same project from a different standpoint. In the schools, however, there was an additional problem. Access for the project team was via the head. Most contact was then with the team leader. But other teachers often loosely attached to the integrated studies team in the school could remain out of contact. Here is one such teacher's complaint on a questionnaire filled in after the end of the trial:

> Leader of the team might have had contact – but *we* didn't. As far as we were concerned Keele didn't exist and I have a feeling they didn't know about us.

This may seem a rather pathetic complaint. But many of these teachers worked hard during the trial. This one was keen enough to fill in a questionnaire and post it. Yet her school was about two miles from the university. If she felt unrecognized most teachers involved in curriculum projects must feel like forgotten lighthouse keepers.

Relations with the Schools Council

The officers of the Schools Council have always insisted that it is a consortium, backed by the local authorities to do work on a national scale, that it is in theory and practice controlled by the teaching profession itself, and that it has no authority over teachers. This combination of characteristics has important implications for the organization and operation of curriculum development. The Schools Council is anxious to avoid the bureaucratization of innovation which would give power to its officers. As a consequence it was very anxious to give as much professional autonomy to its project teams as possible. However, among first-phase projects with no guideline along which to work, this led to difficulties.

The first Schools Council representative on the steering committee of the Keele project was a teacher prominent in the NUT. Only in June 1968, fourteen months after the approval of the project and six months after the appointment of the project team, did the officers of the Schools Council visit Keele. This was partly due to staff turnover at the Schools Council and the amount of work that these officers had to do in the early years once the first phase

of projects had been established. But it was also the attempt to preserve the professional autonomy of project teams. In the case of the
Keele project, however, little information seems to have reached the
Schools Council. The appointed link man was not able to attend
the meetings of the consultative steering committee. Little information appeared to have been received by the Schools Council about
the progress made in the first six months.

To the project team this apparent lack of interest was worrying.
But when the officers of the Schools Council did meet the project
team their report was critical.[15] From being apparently ignored,
the project team now felt that it had been unjustly criticized and
misunderstood as a consequence of the previous lack of contact. At
this meeting in June 1968 one important point emerged. It was confirmed that the Schools Council expected the project to yield
practical help to teachers in the form of teaching materials. This was
confirmation of the direction that had been adopted by the project
team. There were criticisms of the over-ambitious nature of the
writing proposed, but from this point on the future direction of the
project was determined.

Observations of project team meetings in 1969 and 1970 indicated
that the relations between the project team and the Schools Council
were never established in any form satisfactory to both parties. The
team felt vulnerable as a consequence. What the Schools Council
saw as the granting of autonomy was often seen as a lack of interest
by those at Keele. The illustration that follows shows how, in these
circumstances, apparently innocent actions could be seen as sinister.

At a planning meeting of 17 September 1970, the team was shown
for the first time Schools Council Pamphlet No. 7 (1970) called
Integrated Studies in the First Years of Secondary School. This pamphlet
seemed to have been written from reports by Schools Council field
officers. In it were accounts of integrated studies teaching in secondary schools. There were descriptions of both the content and the
organization of this work. This was the first time the project team,
itself concerned with the introduction of integrated studies in the
secondary schools, had seen this pamphlet. There was no reference

to its work.[16] Indeed, the suggestions within the pamphlet violated most of the ideas that were being advanced by the project team, supporting a blurring of subject discipline boundaries as a solution to problems raised by the shock of transfer from primary to secondary school and of apathy in the secondary school, but without any rationale or justification.

In the interviewing programme with Schools Council officers at the end of the project, there was no realization that the publication of this pamphlet had been taken as an affront by the project team. It was seen merely as a way of presenting examples of ongoing work in schools. Indeed, the absence of any discussion of what was being integrated in the examples was deliberate in a pamphlet designed only to give some picture of actual work in schools. But the Integrated Studies Project was itself challenging this approach to integration that ignored thought about objectives.[17] Consequently the pamphlet not only appeared to be a snub, but appeared to undermine the work that was being done. Many examples of such apparent conflicts occur in this book. It will be argued throughout that they are not merely misunderstandings, but different parties in the education system putting forward what they see as legitimate views from their own position. Things look very different once you move from Schools Council to project team to local authority or to schools.

The identity of the project team

The structure envisaged for the project can be seen in Figure 2 (p. 23). The team was to be linked to the schools through the coordinators, and to the local authorities, the teacher organizations and the Schools Council through the advisory committee. It was based in the university that had originally proposed the development. But the communication difficulties listed above indicate the marginal position in which a project team finds itself. It was in the university but not part of it. It was in the schools but not part of them. It worked parallel to but not with local authority advisers. It was financed by the Schools Council, but contacts had been scanty.

In three of the four cases teachers were seconded from the local authority as coordinators. The local authorities still saw them as their teachers. In the early months of the project there was some reluctance to allow them to act independently as full members of the project team. There were considerable gains in having well-known local teachers spreading ideas from Keele into the schools. But the fact that these teachers were known and did not come as outsiders possibly reduced their authority in the schools. This applied particularly in their contacts with headteachers. Certainly the coordinators themselves were faced with conflicting pressures. They came from, and would probably return to, the authority in which they were working. Any difference of opinion between the local authority and the project team placed them in an awkward situation.

The project team was particularly vulnerable in the first months. Initially the team was collecting evidence on ongoing work in the schools. To the teachers this was asking for advice where it had been expected that such advice would be given. To some teachers this was taken to mean that the project knew less about integrated studies than the schools themselves. Later on when the project materials were being shown to the schools for possible trial, the team was seen as inconvenient salesmen. It always takes time to get used to a new job, but when that job takes place outside the organizations with which it is concerned, the feeling of being detached is increased and the chances of being misunderstood are also increased.

This feeling of detachment, of isolation, accounts not only for the feelings of injustice felt by the team when an adverse report was presented by the officers of the Schools Council. Even more important was its effect on the adoption of the idea that curriculum materials should be produced and published. The production of such materials was a job with a clear end-product. It gave the project something that could be offered to the schools in return for their cooperation. It simultaneously satisfied the Schools Council who now asked for materials to be produced and presented an opportunity for the team to ensure that something it had produced would survive beyond the life of the project. In this way the production of publishable materials solved the basic dilemma that had been faced by the team. This dilemma arose out of the vague terms of reference with which it had been presented. In the early months of operation it was not clear to an outsider whether the team was engaged in a feasibility study or in a study that was going to produce curriculum materials to support new courses in the schools. But once the decision to produce materials had been confirmed the fact-finding could cease and production begin.

The time that elapsed between the decision by the Schools Council to support the project in April 1967, and the actual start of the trial of materials in the schools in September 1969, is surprisingly long. Six months had been taken up in political negotiations to decide the constitution of the advisory committee. Another nine months elapsed before the complete team was assembled. By this time the titles of the first five curriculum units had been approved by the advisory committee. By November 1968 the trial schools had been assembled. Pre-trial pilot runs of parts of these materials were introduced experimentally into some schools from September 1968. Thus the first six months of the life of the project team had been spent in determining where it wanted to go and how it was going to get there. The next six months were spent in assembling rough drafts of the curriculum units and in persuading schools to try these out. In the nine months that remained before the trial began in September 1969 these curriculum units were written and revised in the light of comments from the schools. This left only one year in which the materials could be tried out in the schools. In May 1969 a proposal was made for an extension to the end of the school year in 1971. The project team now knew where it wanted to go. It had established firm links with a limited number of schools. It had learned to live in a marginal position, and to simultaneously satisfy the demands from the schools for usable materials and the requests from the Schools Council that these be produced for publication.

The importance of the production of curriculum materials for publication in solving problems for development teams may account for this becoming the usual procedure. Early communications between Keele and the Schools Council before the project team was appointed stressed curriculum development based on the university as a centre for regional and local initiatives. The original written proposals for the Integrated Studies Project contained no mention of curriculum packs. But once materials had been produced their trial and improvement became the primary aim of the team in its relation with the schools. By 1971 when the pressure from the publishers was felt the team was spending most of its time sorting out packs into publishable form. It is difficult to sustain any effort when there is little tangible outcome. The production of materials was satisfying, provided a measurable output and ensured that the ideas of the team would survive and spread. The final published version of these packs justifies this concentration of effort and ensures that the momentum of dissemination will be sustained. The Schools Council seems to have come to expect that there would be publication. But the production of materials for publication may be as much a solution to the uncertainties over procedure in curriculum development teams as a response to needs detected in the schools.

The uncertainty over procedures resulted from the absence of any national or local strategy for introducing and supporting change. Local authority initiatives and Schools Council projects coexisted in the same schools but each was seen by the teachers as a separate development. Within the schools there was no attempt to plan support for innovation. Similarly the local authorities supported specific projects but only sporadic attempts were made to relate one development to another or provide a fertile soil for all. The Integrated Studies Project existed at the same time as the Moral Education, Environmental Studies and Humanities Schools Council projects. Occasionally there was friction. Never in the schools studied here was there any attempt to see a project or a combination of projects, whether initiated by the Schools Council or local advisers, as involving the whole school in planned change involving all the staff. To the detached observer the chance of survival seemed slight, not because of any shortcomings in the innovation but because each set of changes was allowed to occur without consideration of the effects on the rest of the curriculum. The interviews with local authority advisers showed that some planning had been done. But the objective was rather to insulate the innovation as an insurance against temporary disruption in the schools than to ensure implementation. An explanation of this apparent lack of enthusiasm for innovation was sought therefore in the various agencies responsible for promoting, supervising and evaluating change.

The setting up and life of the project has been illustrated by Bolam (1973) in Figure 3.

The partners	Stage one Negotiation	Stage two Development	Stage three Publication	Stage four Implementation
University Institute of Education				
Project team		Full team	One member only	
Local Education Authorities			Own developments	
Trial schools			Own developments	
Publishers	When best starting point ?			
Schools Council				

Figure 3 *Partners in the project*

This diagram offers an overview of the main partners in the project and the main stages in which they are concerned. The thick line shows when a particular partner was directly and actively involved. The broken line is intended to show when they were either partially involved, or were undertaking work similar in kind to that advocated by the project but acting separately and on their own initiative. Among possible points for reflection are:

1. *The partners involved most briefly were:*
   (a) *The team. Full team was financed for three years and eight months, and the Director continued for one further year.*
   (b) *The trial schools. Most were involved across two trial years, but several had experimented with integrated studies before the project, and most continued to develop it, in their own styles, after the project finished.*

Even if the life of the project had been increased, the main point would still stand: a curriculum development project, and the trial schools in their formal relationships to it have a limited existence.

2. *The two institutions with the most long-term concern for the development of integrated studies are:*

   (a) *The Institute of Education, University of Keele. The project arose out o, the university's pioneer interest in interdisciplinary studies, expressed in its Foundation Year Course. The Institute of Education has a curriculum/ integrated studies component, both in its in-service courses and in those of its constituent colleges.*
   (b) *The Schools Council. The interest of the Council began from the original negotiations before the formation of the team, continued throughout the project, and will go on as part of its overall concern to promote knowledge and support of the curriculum developments which it has initiated. In working practice, the project was not always dealing with the same individuals. This is partly because key personnel changed, but also because the nature of the work varied and contact was made with a different department, e.g. field officers, evaluation team, publications secretary, finance, etc.*

◆◆ Comments by D. R. Jenkins

[1] My clear impression here was that the local authorities were hard pressed to defend on principle their general feeling that an already cumbersome committee could become more cumbersome if the teachers' representation increased. Perhaps also there was the suspicion that the committee could become a forum for purely domestic disputes.

[2] There was some confusion between an advisory and a research role. This led to the first major dispute within the team. One co-ordinator seemed to be indulging a taste for an advisory role, rather than coolly collecting information about practices and issues as perceived by teachers.

[3] There were some spectacular mishaps, left out of official accounts. In particular, a proposed pack on Change fell just victim to the concept it focused on! Some of these early proposals were over-hurried and consequently ill considered.

[4] A promise not really fulfilled. Although one coordinator became the project's information- retrieval man, and did quite a lot of work on identifying the key concepts embedded in individual items of material, the wider task was scarcely attempted. Neither did the coordinate indexing get off the ground except in one trial school.

[5] Except in schools. The policy of recruitment was a grassroots one, based on good work done in the classroom (see also Chapter 8 by Bolam, p. 140).

[6] The only heavy involvement was my own in running the Curriculum Theory and Practice course for the Advanced Diploma. This contributed to my own heavily theoretical orientation to the project's central tasks. On reflection, I probably over-dramatized this assumed role as the project's gateway-man to the curriculum literature. In any case the notion was less than endearing given the coordinators' self-doubt in this area of study and the problems of marginality posed at Keele.

[7] The teachers' centre proposals took on the flavour of a political dispute, the central theme of which was whether the Keele Institute of Education was guilty of opportunistic encroachment on a local education authority preserve.

[8] In spite of the pious aspirations, I am not able to say whether the resource centre actually opened in September 1969. All I can say is that if it did the Assistant Director had no idea where it was physically located. The suggestion was made that the purchasing of equipment could be made to tie up with the existing facilities at Keele (see also Chapter 8 by Bolam, pp. 143–4).

[9] This lapse in memory may be deliberate. At least one local authority used the project as monkey-gland injections to rejuvenate tired schools, while at the same time protecting its own successful innovative schools like virtuous daughters. Teachers commonly thought that project schools could attract both money and prestige over and above capitation and routine praise.

[10] This point has serious and critical implications. It is in the knowledge of these that I concede its accuracy.

[11] These coordinators' reports, although on a tight brief, varied wildly in tone and content.

[12] *Mea culpa.* The only alternative, however, was for the project to do its conceptual thinking in private. Teachers see jargon as the perverse elaboration of simple ideas rather than as a way of thinking. The unspoken rebuke was that Keele had over-generously set up the chance of ego trips for project members and prestigious outsiders. When a professor of education gave a sharply theoretical talk to the inaugural conference, a wag was heard to call out, 'Is there a teacher in the house?'

[13] My counterplay to this one lies in the feedback forms themselves, which seem unexceptional. I think that teachers pressed for time may easily have neglected feedback but felt the need to rationalize the 'breach of contract' by questioning the value of the rules, always the more defensible stance for the deviant to take!

[14] This led to a shift in emphasis towards participant observation as the chief source of feedback, and put further pressures on the already overworked coordinators.

[15] The Director and the Assistant Director discussed the report and decided not to agenda it at a team meeting because it was highly critical, in purely personal terms, of one member of the team. The basis of these adverse judgements was less than clear, and seemed to be based on a quick intuitive judgement by one of the Schools Council field officers. Although the relationship with the field officers was subsequently improved, the early days were characterized by mutual suspicion. The sense of unjust criticism arose out of the inspectorial tone of the visitors. It was a reaction to style as much as a reaction to content.

[16] The unanimous view of the project team was that Schools Council Pamphlet No. 7 was irredeemably lightweight. Had it borrowed freely from project thinking any plagiarism would have been gratefully overlooked. But its silence was read as dismissive, and I think correctly, even after reading this chapter. Its own very intellectual sloppiness in these circumstances added insult to injury. Similarly the Henbury School Project was set up ostensibly to build on and relate to Keele, but the Schools Council failed to formalize links.

[17] This comment is misleading. The project certainly avoided a 'behavioural objectives' paradigm and there was, for example, no attempt to use Bloom's *Taxonomy of Educational Objectives* (1956) as a basis for categorizing the objectives to be evaluated. An approach to integration through objectives could imply that the project saw integration as a means towards preordinate ends, rather than as an alternative method of organizing a curriculum in need of further understanding before responsible choices can be made.

3. Contrasting interpretations and definitions

In this chapter the focus is on the way the various agents involved in the Keele Integrated Studies Project defined their part in it. These definitions were detected through the interviewing programme which spanned the years from 1969 to 1972. This programme, by covering not only the various parties involved, but through observing and interviewing across three years, enabled changes in definition among the various parties to be traced and related.

The accounts that follow are over-simplifications of the positions taken. Within each group there were a number of contrasting views. It is misleading to think that there is a clear definition of a curriculum project from the start. Even the project team had to establish objectives, definitions and modes of operation. These objectives were modified as the project progressed. The definitions of the curriculum project came as problems of design, introduction into schools, implementation, publication and diffusion were met and overcome. Similarly definitions by the teachers, headteachers, field officers and advisers changed as the project developed. In all cases there was first the emergence of a definition and then modification. In every case this definition and modification were achieved through interaction with other groups. Curriculum change does not proceed through a clear cycle from a statement of objectives to an evaluation of the learning strategies used. It is a process of bargaining, negotiation and horse-trading.

Some of this suspicion arose from threats felt by teachers accepting a trial in their schools. This was most apparent wherever evaluation was discussed. The teachers felt incompetent as integrated studies was new to them. In early meetings at Keele teachers asked what was going to be evaluated, the project or their teaching. The project team wanted evaluation to start as the trial started, but teachers wanted time to settle down first. The Schools Council seemed unconcerned and finally refused to finance evaluation. In the first term of trial in 1969 coordinators at team meetings reported concern about evaluation of work in trial schools being available to local authority advisers. As the second year of trial was being planned the tendency of teachers to exclude coordinators from their planning meetings was discussed by the project team. The suspicion can be summed up by the remark of one headteacher that he did not want a parade of researchers stuffing thermometers into his staff.

This suspicion was found in relations between project team, teachers, headteachers and local authority advisers. It was aggravated by the difficulties in communicating across local authority boundaries. A course in area X could not be attended by teachers in area Y. The coordinator in area W could not go into schools in area V. But the coordinators, sensitive to the feelings of local teachers, reduced suspicion by protecting their schools from excessive research and from any excessive demands of evaluation. More centralized projects would not have this means of detecting and reducing hostility. The absence of local coordinators would probably mean that they would never be aware of the tension that actually existed in the field.

The project team

The project was initially defined by the central team as a cooperative exercise in exploring the problems and possibilities of integration in the humanities. It was to be an invitation to schools to join in an experiment, not to try out a new syllabus. The organization of the project team, with coordinators linking schools to each other and to the centre, was designed for the joint production and trials of materials. Broad guidelines were to be provided, but each school was to experiment within these. The type of phrase used in early documents on the project included 'serving growth points' and 'to service and support innovations in humanities teaching in secondary schools'.

This cooperative venture rested on efficient feedback. Schedules were provided to ease the task of the teachers in sending back accounts of the use and evaluation of materials. Suggestions were made about suitable methods of testing, assessing, recording and reviewing children's work. Throughout, the teachers were seen as partners and the original plans centred on a teachers' centre where materials could be jointly developed. Coordinators who were members of the project team at Keele, but working in the schools, were paid by the local authorities involved, and were to be the agents for mobilizing the teachers into the innovation.

In the early documents sent to potential trial schools, it was stressed that integration was not a stitching together of existing subjects to make one all-over blanket of knowledge. The concern was to introduce children to subjects, seen as ways of understanding. Subjects were to be used as tools of enquiry. Integration, far from being the mixing up of subjects, was to be seen as a method of using subjects with distinctive procedures, concepts and methods of verification. It was to be a planned exercise involving different ways of finding out. This view of integration was first advanced in 1968, and remained the basic principle behind the Integrated Studies Project throughout its life.

The teachers

While integrated studies was new to most schools in 1968, many had been experimenting with forms of humanities teaching. Of the thirty-eight schools involved at some time between 1968 and 1971, twenty-two were already experimenting in this field before joining the trial. In two local authority areas there was a move to introduce humanities with the active support of the local authority advisers. These schools, which were already experimenting, tended to become the trial schools. Thus adaptation accompanied innovation.

A common perspective of all teachers in the thirty-eight schools was of a project to be used to develop tailor-made courses. The project was seen as a support for humanities teaching, particularly in view of the imminent raising of the school leaving age. This school-centred view of the project contrasted starkly with the idea of a trial of new content and methods for possible diffusion elsewhere.

This can be seen most clearly in the schools' response to early documents from the project stressing that integration did not mean fitting together bits from different subjects but rather meant utilizing the unique contribution of those individual subjects. Few schools seemed to grasp this idea or even consider it. Even after two years of trial most were proud of their success in breaking down the boundaries between subjects. Consequently team teaching, which was recommended as a method of organization, was usually seen, not as a way of using specialists, but as a way of producing general teachers. Indeed one of the complaints about the hard work that was involved in innovation came from the perceived need to act simultaneously as historian, geographer, social scientist, biologist and so on. This misunderstanding was possible because few of the teachers involved had understood or even bothered to read the sections of documents produced by the team that related to the principles of integration. Integrated studies was taken to mean integrated teachers rather than integrated subject disciplines, despite the clear policy statements by the Project Director and team (Bolam 1972).[1]

The tendency of the teachers to accept the project as something to be adapted to conditions in their own schools resulted in thirty-eight different projects. Each school highlighted the aspects that suited the teachers involved. This may have accounted for the very low priority given to providing feedback to the project, even though the schools had committed themselves to this work at the start and were under continual pressure from the project team once they had started. Only two of the thirty-eight schools provided regular feedback. Only nineteen regularly attended meetings. The reasons given by the teachers were that they were too busy as a result of the innovation to use up more time filling in forms or going to Keele. But this was not just a gap in communications. The definitions of the project team and of the teachers were at different levels. The teachers were involved in their own problems and defined the project out of their own experience in their own classrooms. As a consequence the basic principles behind the project were usually misunderstood and often unconsidered.

The project team was well aware of this difficulty from an early date. The coordinators soon took over the job of ensuring feedback by actually collecting it in the schools. The coordinators also translated the principles of the project into terms that were meaningful to individual teachers in schools facing individual problems. There was, however, an important exception to the parochial view taken by the teachers. The project was a powerful support for those who wanted to innovate. Curiously, in the interviews, the teachers not only praised the project team for the support they provided through the provision of materials and advice on teaching strategy, but stressed how useful were the ideas advanced. But these ideas seen as useful were about themes, topics, materials and teaching methods, rather than about underlying principles. Their usefulness was derived from the support that the label 'Keele' could provide. This acted rather like the 'by appointment to the Queen' cachet that guarantees the quality of other products. When these teachers came under pressure from other staff in the schools, they could claim the support of Keele for what they were doing.

The local authority advisers

Trial schools from six local authority areas were involved in the project. The salaries of the coordinators were paid by four of these authorities. The local advisory staff varied in the responsibility they took in determining which schools should join and the extent of their commitment. Similarly the local authorities varied in the way they defined the expected role of the coordinators. In two authorities the coordinators were given complete freedom. In another authority the coordinator was under pressure in the first trial year from the local advisory staff to adapt to the developing pattern of humanities teaching already existing and developing in the schools. In the fourth local authority area the coordinator was seen as remaining one of the teachers of that authority. The local authority advisory staff were protective towards their schools. They saw the project as a temporary influence only. Yet they had continuing responsibility for school policy. They did not want a temporary, radical change that would disturb existing developments or start others that would be left in the lurch when the trial ended. They were willing to provide support, but they were careful to limit the commitment of schools where they thought over-engagement could be damaging once the trial period ended.

The project was defined therefore as a means to ends that the advisers saw as their long-term responsibility. One local authority adviser put it this way:

> I have responsibility for these schools until the end of the century. The project will exist for two years only. If teachers go overboard on integrated studies and then at the end of two years find that it is not suitable, they will lose confidence in their ability to change things and I will have lost a lot of the goodwill and initiative which has been built up over the years.

This view was shared by all the advisory staff interviewed. But the action that they based upon it varied. At one extreme the project was seen and used as a lever to produce changes in various schools in directions determined by the advisory staff. Schools were selected in the hope that they would change as a result of being involved in the trial, while other schools were chosen because they were changing, but, in the opinion of the advisory staff, in the wrong direction. These were explicable views, given the long-term perspectives of the advisers. But it destroyed the randomness of the sample of trial schools. Once again, here was another definition of the curriculum situation. At the other extreme there were advisory staff who did not intervene actively. They merely kept a watching brief to ensure that certain developments were not disturbed within the two trial years. This attitude was a result of the absence of development work in the field of the humanities in these areas. In the two areas where such developments were going on, the advisers played a very active part in selecting schools and determining the limits of innovation. In three areas where there was little development in the humanities, intervention in the work of the project was very slight.

There were occasions where local authority advisory staff took a more active part in influencing the implementation of the project. This applied particularly in the early days of the trial in 1969 and early 1970. A curriculum project does not deliver the goods fully packaged to trial schools. It develops the work as a consequence of experience gained. This was a worry for the advisory staff who had overall responsibility for the schools. Where teaching in the humanities had been developing under their guidance the project could seem a threat. The stronger the tide of change before the trial period the more likely was this kind of conflict. But there were clashes where there was apparently no overlap. Advisers felt the project was interfering with the local development of sex education in 1969 and at the end of the project with ROSLA plans. These conflicts led to the coordinators being in a difficult position. But their very existence was also an advantage. They could rapidly feed back to the project centre any feelings of distrust felt in the local authority areas.

The Schools Council

It was not possible to detect a Schools Council definition of this project. This was partly because the Schools Council is not a unitary body and there were many officers involved with this project across its life. It was also because the Schools Council deliberately aimed at granting autonomy to the project team. Nevertheless there was one very significant conflict between the Schools Council on one hand and the local advisory staff on the other, which recurred through advisory committee meetings from 1969 to 1971. There was no change in this conflict, it merely became more marked, and if anything more strongly argued. The local advisory staff, usually supported by the teachers, argued in advisory committee meetings that the Schools Council organized national projects to impose ideas on schools. The Keele project was seen as an example of this. This was vigorously denied by Schools Council personnel, who maintained that this was a project designed to develop work already going on at grassroots level, and out of that experience to develop curriculum materials that would be of use outside the trial schools area.

There seemed to be no way of reconciling these two views. Each was generated within a different context. The advisory staff, and the teachers, judged the use made of the resources given to the project by reference to the pay-off in their schools. The view of the Schools Council officers, and of the project team, was that the benefit from the investment would be spread nationally over a longer period of time. This difference of definition resulted in different criteria being used in evaluating the success of the project. The Schools Council and the project team were in no position to judge the success of the exercise at the end of the trial period in 1971. The teachers and the local advisory staff, however, were in such a position because they were judging success at the local level. This view was expressed at the final meeting of the advisory committee. A tribute was paid to the work of the project team and its benefit to the local schools acknowledged. This tribute was based on the report of an observers' panel consisting of local authority advisers and college of education lecturers who had investigated the impact of the project in the local schools. But the glow generated by this tribute was rapidly cooled by teachers and advisers saying that next time it would be better to give the money to the local schools to develop their own work. Yet to the Schools Council and project team this had been one of the main aims of the exercise. Indeed, their complaint was that the schools did not show enough initiative and were reluctant to feed their experiences back to the project. This advisory committee had met over a period of three years. Yet even at the end the definitions used by the parties represented came out of such different contexts that they still conflicted. Each party recognized the particular difficulties of the other. But when decisions had to be made over policy the same situation appeared very different from local and national perspectives.

It may be that curriculum development projects have to live with such conflicting definitions. Certainly at Keele there was no difficulty in making policy decisions, even though there was this fundamental underlying difference of definition. But this was achieved by concentrating on procedures not principles, means not ends. The net impact of the project was the result of the interaction of the different and changing perceptions of the groups involved. Each group, indeed each school, had separate, even idiosyncratic aims. It may be therefore, that conventional evaluations are a waste of time. They are designed to test the impact of a project against a universal predetermined list of objectives, but impact from the viewpoint of those involved is judged at a particular, local, level. Very often this local impact will consist of changes judged to be important by those involved in the schools, but not anticipated or even perceived by those at the centre, and certainly not defined as objectives by them. The accidental pay-offs may turn out to be of more importance to trial schools, although the predicted results may be more significant for the national impact. This point is discussed fully in Chapter 7. It can be anticipated here through the remarks by enthusiastic teachers and heads, who said that they had benefited greatly from the trial exercise, but then spelled out reasons for this enthusiasm which were certainly not anticipated, and probably would have horrified the project team.

Changes in definition

Definitions of curricula arise not only out of different contexts but out of changes in personnel and organization. Within the two years of trial, 1968 to 1971, two of the five local authority advisers, a member of the project team, the original Schools Council field officer in the area and two successive Schools Council joint secretaries responsible for the project moved to other jobs. Staff turnover in schools was high. One local authority reorganized its secondary schooling and two other areas had started to implement their plans. For many schools this reorganization was a reason for deferring further innovation. But even where there was little reorganization across the years of the project there was considerable redefinition by the parties involved.

The first set of redefinitions came as exact terms of reference were sorted out. The project was originally suggested as part of the programme for raising the school leaving age in 1968. When this was put off, the brief was given to the project team without limits on the age range or subjects to be included. But local authority advisers still tended to see the project as preparation for a longer secondary schooling while the project team designed a trial for the eleven to sixteen year olds.

The project team also seemed to have swung the emphasis from humanities to integrated studies. Advisory committee minutes were headed 'Keele Humanities Project' in September 1968, inviting confusion with the other Schools Council project in this area. In November 1968 minutes were titled 'Project for the Integration of the Humanities'. In January 1970 the advisory committee approved the title 'Integrated Studies Project'. To outsiders this confirmed the new priority to integration. Pressure for such a change in title had come from Stenhouse, the Director of the Schools Council Humanities Project, who served on the advisory committee at Keele This may have avoided confusion nationally, but the switch in emphasis, which seemed to be only a change of title to the project team, was seen by local authority advisers as confirmation that the project was avoiding giving them help with their most pressing problem of preparing new courses for the extra year. [2]

The second redefinition revolved around the organization of the project. To cope with its work the project team had to concentrate more on its efforts at Keele. In the second trial year of 1970–1 less contact was needed with schools since the necessary information had already been collected. A few schools were trying out new material and were visited frequently, but as the trial moved to its end most schools felt that contact with the project team diminished.

The teachers detected this centralization of the project at the same time as they were thinking of the work they would do after the end of the trial. Already they had altered materials and procedures to suit the conditions in and around their schools. While the project was being centralized to finish the job in time, integrated studies in schools was being localized.

The local authority advisers adopted a detached and sceptical view of these contrasting shifts. The caution of the local authority advisory staff relaxed as the project turned out to be benign in its influence. The moves in the schools to localize the work were supported. Early anxieties evaporated once it was clear that integrated studies could be assimilated into the school curriculum without disturbance. There was no active intervention by the advisers in the second year of trial. By the end of the trial period the project was viewed as one more innovation that had served as a useful catalyst, one more piece in a strategy that was always being put together. Indeed, the project team was baffled by the apparent lack of interest in the outcome, not only by the local authorities but also by the Schools Council itself. Just as the project team reached the finale, its sponsor and audience seemed to lose interest.[3]

C

However, this progressive detachment of the advisers was accompanied by scepticism. They saw the centralization as confirmation that planned curriculum projects imposed ideas on their schools. They also saw it as a retreat from their problem with the less able pupil, particularly once the leaving age was raised. From the start they had strongly criticized the project team for producing materials that were too difficult for the children and advice for teachers that was too abstract. The centralization of the project to produce these materials for publication was seen by them as the final proof that their early suspicion was justified. They complained as the trial in schools started in October 1969 that the production of curriculum materials for publication was unnecessary. They maintained this criticism to the finish in 1971. This jaundiced view of the advisers was directed more against curriculum projects in general than Keele in particular. Indeed, the advisers formed a half of the observers' panel set up to evaluate the work in the trial schools, and this group produced a favourable report in 1971 as the second year of trial neared its end. They acknowledged that the trial school children and teachers had benefited. They also saw the experience of trial as a useful guide for future developments in their area. But they still thought that they could have obtained better results if they had been given the money. Their priority was the success of their schools. The project team was aiming to spread integrated studies beyond the trial areas.

The final redefinition was unexpected and macabre. The most striking difference in definition during the trial was the teachers' attempts to become general, multi-subject experts in the face of the project team's stress on the need to maintain subject disciplines in the team teaching situation. In the interviews with teachers in the terms following the end of the trial they were apologetic about changing back to their subject role. They saw this as backsliding from what they assumed was the style supported by Keele. Yet in reality they were moving back to just the role that the project team had been trying to get them to adopt for two years previously. When this anomaly was pointed out to them the teachers expressed surprise but insisted that the project team had wanted them to be integrated teachers.[4]

One explanation for this comedy of errors may have been that there is general pressure for teachers to break down subject boundaries. Local authority advisers supported this style of integration. The project team may have been misunderstood because integration is a slogan in widespread use and the team was using it in a more sophisticated way than do sociologists and curriculum theorists who support integration but rarely define it. The failure of teachers to read or understand the theoretical handouts by the team would make this explanation feasible. But this is guesswork, not interpretation. No agreement emerged from those interviewed.

Some idea of the difference between the project view of the teaching role and that adopted by the teachers can be gauged by the following quotations. The first is from a guide to schools prepared by the project team in 1968:

Integration is not seen as soldering together existing subjects, or any variant of them, to make one master blueprint of knowledge. The concern is to introduce children to subjects, seen as ways of understanding, which collectively can help them explore large issues and themes.

In 1969 this version was still being pressed in project handouts:

It will be important to ensure that a teacher's particular *subject expertise* is fully used, however much integrated work widens his personal interests and calls on him for general oversight of children's work.

In 1972, Bolam, the Project Director, was still having to warn that integration had been seen not as a way of 'adding together diverse pieces of information, but as the planned cooperation between different ways of finding out'. Yet despite this remarkable consistency in definition across the years of the project, the teachers persisted in claiming that breaking down subject boundaries and specialist perspectives was what had been wanted. The final word came from a headteacher in a most successful trial school. When this school was visited after the end of the trial an imaginative scheme of work in junior forms had been organized out of the work with Keele. The head summed it up like this:

> I give full credit to Keele for the ideas they have given us. But it's my staff who finally worked it all out. They did the work, Now we don't present packets of knowledge to the children, we are all ready to spread over subject boundaries. Even subjects like social science that were new to us. Flexible sums it up. It's natural for the children. Later they will be ready for subjects but we're delaying the dividing up as late as possible.

◆◆ Comments by D. R. Jenkins and Geoffrey Hartley

[1] This is acutely interesting. It undermines the whole concept of 'a cooperative exercise in exploring the problems and possibilities of integration in the humanities'. But surely there is a sense in which the 'problems' come out of the possibilities as these are properly understood in context. Anything else is a retreat to off-the-cuff consideration of immediate snags. The issues relate logically to the rationale. Shipman's point also calls into question the usefulness of the project's view that theme-based teaching in the humanities 'is best taught by the concerted action of a group of teachers'. The means have been mistaken for the ends. [D. J.]

[2] I find this point very surprising indeed. The change in project title was to avoid straightforward confusion with the Humanities Curriculum Project. The emotional halo surrounding the word 'humanities' may suggest ROSLA work, but the project had always linked the two concepts (i.e. integration in the humanities). Although its view of the humanities area was unusually wide, this much

was clear before the change in title. If the local authority advisers saw the project as preparation for longer secondary schooling, this starkly contrasted with a number of separate attempts by Schools Council personnel on the advisory committee to advise the project to limit its interest to the so-called junior packs. The Schools Council was later able, by a happy coincidence, to negotiate a deal with the Oxford University Press, which committed initially both parties to publish junior packs only (see also Chapter 8 by Bolam, pp. 165-6). [D. J.]

[3] I find this a delightful comment, expressing exactly the views of the coordinators. Two points surprised us at the time. First, there was the apparent lack of ultimate interest by local education authorities and Schools Council, in spite of the considerable financial outlay. Second, there was the failure to cash in on the expertise of the project team gained over the trial years. [G. H.]

[4] A rare over-simplification. I do not think it true that in any crude sense the project wanted subject specialists teaching in teams. There were real differences in emphasis within the team on this one, and 'project' documents tended to reflect individual viewpoints. The whole point about team teaching is that individual teachers play a variety of roles (e.g. chairman of stable discussion groups) and are expected themselves to acquire an 'integrated' overview of the theme, topic or problem as well as offer specialist skills, concepts and modes of enquiry. Neither do I recall teachers taking a simplistic opposite view, seeing themselves merely as generalists. The dichotomy is an artificial one anyway, once a decision has been taken to use an organizing category for the curriculum that is itself supra-subject. [D. J.]

4. Pressures on the project team

At the start of work on the project in the schools, neither the project team nor the teachers had any clear idea of the labour that was involved in curriculum innovation. At the start of the project when the results were not coming through and the work load was at its greatest, the extra work did not seem to be producing compensating rewards. Later on the curriculum materials started to appear in finished form and the curriculum development team got the first taste of public recognition. But in the early stages of the project both for the project team and for the teachers, this kind of reward was missing and frustration was common. It was this lack that made the question of the work load involved so important.

This frustration is reduced once work has begun on producing curriculum materials. Here there are tangible results for effort. But the process of writing and distributing materials and of convincing schools that the materials are worth a trial and then evaluating their use inevitably produces more waste. For every page that was finally published there were probably a dozen that finally ended in the waste paper basket. They proved to be either unsuitable, superfluous to requirements, or irrelevant once the original theme of the curriculum materials changed over time. The author of a book makes the decisions over what to include himself. The authors of curriculum materials are dependent on the teachers and the children making these decisions for them. Many of their brightest ideas turn out to be damp squibs once they go into the schools. The project team has to stand the strain of seeing its ideas used in ways that it may not approve, and finally often criticized and rejected by the teachers.

A new set of problems arrived once the project team started to produce public documents and became a centre of attention. The Keele project started off with a simple division of labour. The Director and Assistant Director would work at Keele, circulating round the trial schools and gathering up information from across the country. The coordinators would link the project headquarters to the trial schools. But this simple division of labour was soon to prove inadequate. As the work piled up at Keele the only solution was for members of the project team to specialize further. Someone had to become primarily responsible for evaluation. Someone else had to become responsible for arranging copyrights. Another had to devise a system for resource storage. Another had to be concerned with diffusion. There were curriculum units to write and try out in the schools, and the specialist interests of the project team were used so that someone took responsibility for the development of a particular unit.

These internal developments, slowly taking up more and more time and calling for more and more specialized interests, were accompanied by an unanticipated increase in work from demands originating outside the project. Many of these demands meant extra work for the project team. They steadily built up the work at Keele, and cut down the amount of time that could be spent in the schools. As early as October 1969, a month after the trial in schools started, local authority advisers were saying in the advisory committee that the team was spending too little time in the schools. This was not a deliberate decision by the project team. It was the result of mounting pressure to provide information and help to people who saw the project as interesting and wanted information about it. It was a form of diffusion.[1] But it also meant that before the work in the trial schools was fully established, energy was having to be deflected to unanticipated demands from other schools, colleges and departments of education, professional associations, international organizations and other local and national interests.

Only the flavour, not the amount of this work can be given here. Projects of a different size and with a different organization would be able to solve this problem in different ways. Nevertheless it always exists. It is in the nature of innovation to attract attention, but to pay attention and provide information involves time. A few examples will have to suffice:

1 As soon as the project was established there was a continuous request from people wishing to visit. These requests were to visit not only the project to see the materials that were being developed, but to visit the trial schools to see the project in action. Each visitor had to be met and accompanied round the schools. These came primarily from colleges and departments of education and often involved large groups of students. But they also came from the inspectorate and advisory services, from publishers, from researchers, from the Schools Council and from overseas visitors.

2 There was a steady build-up in the request for information by post and telephone. Much of this was routine and could be answered without involving the project team. But much of it required the attention of the team member specializing in the field of interest. For example, as the development of materials progressed, the negotiations over copyright became important and time consuming. But this also meant that much more care had to be taken over the referencing of materials. One team member had to become responsible for working out an adequate reference system for all materials in use. Postage and telephone bills also became a considerable item of expense for the project.

3 The Keele project was based in an institute of education. Inevitably the pressure built up to use the experience of the project to establish courses within that Institute. The first course was in curriculum theory. This was organized as an advanced diploma course by the Director and Assistant Director. But the colleges of education within the ATO were also interested and set up their own courses, asking for help from the project team. By the end of the project one of these colleges had become a major centre for

the development of work in the humanities and was working very closely with the project team. This work in teacher training and in-service courses was an important part of diffusion, but this lecturing load and support service was time consuming.

4 It was not only permanent courses that took up time in lecturing and the preparation of courses. The members of the project team were in demand as visiting speakers for conferences, colleges of education and departments of education. This demand built up steadily during the trial years 1969 to 1971. It persisted beyond the life of the project. Such conferences were a useful way of spreading the ideas being formulated and could not easily be rejected. But they were, once again, time consuming and demand was at a peak just as the amount of work was at its maximum in the production and testing of materials.

5 Across the life of the project, five overseas fellows were attached. These overseas fellows were from West and East Africa. They mostly came for one year, which was spent with the project, with visits to schools and to colleges of education. Since returning to Africa, they have been responsible for setting up curriculum development in the humanities. Their presence with the project, was again time consuming. The work of these overseas fellows was crucial in the development of a curriculum unit on Development in Africa. They played a valuable part as members of the central team. Their evaluation of the work of the project was useful, but their presence stretched the work of the project team beyond the original terms of reference and increased the strain on individuals.[2]

6 Negotiations over possible publishing had started in early 1969. By late 1969 the three junior packs had been accepted for publication, at least in principle. There was interest in the three senior packs, but no decision had been made, as the trial of these was not yet advanced. As the packs were developed the amount of time that had to be spent organizing for publishing increased. In a way this can be seen as the means through which a project ensures that its work will persist. The decision to publish materials was a

crucial one. It fixed the direction of the project's work. It provided a target and motivation, but it also involved the team in rewriting and editing.

The actual negotiations with the publishers were not too time consuming. But the preparation of the material for publication became a major concern. As the pressure to complete the project's work in time increased, so the pressure to produce materials for publication by deadlines increased. From the moment that a decision to publish materials was made, there was another timetable in existence for the project. There was then a need to synchronize the trial of materials in schools, with the need to get these written up in a publishable form.

There were two complications as the team started to prepare materials for publication. They were both derived from the short time that is available for trial, feedback and evaluation in two years of trial when publishing was an objective from early days. In order to make the finished product available so that schools could take up the work as the trial ended, publishing problems had to be solved while materials were still being tried and amended.

The first problem was a direct consequence of this rush. Differences of opinion over suitability for publication inevitably arose between project team and publisher. This was not just a clash between academic and commercial interests but arose from difficulties over defining the market. The publishers wanted materials suitable for a wide range of abilities, including children with poor reading ability. The project team had a continuing difficulty in producing materials that were usable at this level.[3] They saw this problem of the poor reader as soluble not through simplified materials but through selective use by the teachers involved. This difference of opinion was frequently concentrated on a section seen by the team as crucial for the whole. There was rarely enough information on use in trial schools to settle the issue. Bolam (1972) has stressed that this problem was three-sided. The team lacked expertise in the publishing world. The publishers had difficulty coming to terms with the principles of integration developed by the team. Consequently the Schools Council was twice called in to arbitrate over the suitability of particular parts of a unit.

The most serious difference of opinion was over the timing of publication. There were six units, half for younger and half for older secondary pupils. The publishers wanted to prepare the three junior packs first and reserved judgement on the senior packs. They argued that it was best to await the response to the junior packs before making a decision. But they supported this by pointing out that the senior packs, having been prepared last, had been given least trial. The project team was divided. One view was that the six units were an inseparable package. A guarantee was needed that all would be published before the junior packs were handed over. The other view was that it was reasonable for the finished and tested junior packs to be published first and for a decision on the remainder deferred.

This was often a bitter conflict within the project team. It was aggravated by the order in which the curriculum units had been accepted as ready for publication. The first to be accepted had been prepared by coordinators. While playing an apparently secondary role they had temporarily produced the only immediately publishable products. This dispute coincided with a period of worry for the coordinators when they were unable to obtain the sort of future post that they would have liked. The rewards for the team seemed to have gone awry. The problem was never settled during the remaining life of the project. But the end of the trial period and the departure of members of the team for other jobs took the steam out of it. It is possible that all projects must experience these difficulties. The Schools Council Humanities Project's pack on Race is only the most publicized example.

The second complication was technical. The production of multi-media materials in a suitable and attractive form for schools is a new enterprise. The project team found it difficult to prune its work to the limitations imposed by cost and production techniques. But the publishers too were feeling their way. This meant more work than is involved in producing a textbook. It was to take a lot of the time of the project team as the project neared its end. It would have been impossible to prepare the senior packs for publication within the life of the project even if this had been agreed with the publisher. The lesson that emerged was clear. Here as elsewhere the project team had no idea how much work was involved at the start of the project. In retrospect too much was probably attempted in too short a time. But there was no way of knowing this at the start for there was little experience of the job that had to be done to serve as a guide to new curriculum development teams to use.

These are only examples of many pressures that built up on the project team across the life of the project. However, they proved to be as much a solution to problems as the cause of them. Once the trial of curriculum materials in schools had started there was little time to do anything but carry on with their development as quickly as possible. Early papers on principles and procedures gave way to meeting publishing deadlines. Even with an extension to the end of the school year in 1971 there was still very little time to complete the work that was seen to be needed to be done. The end of the project coincided with the end of the school year. At this point all the evaluation, all the writing, all the diffusion had to be complete. A project generates its own momentum. There is an acceleration towards the end of the life of the project, but inevitably many loose ends remain to be tied. In the case of the Keele project this was accomplished by the Director staying with the work for an extra year into 1972. But it is a comment on the difficulties of establishing projects for a limited period of three years. It would be a miracle if the different strands of the work were all tied up at the terminal date.[4]

It was this mounting pressure of work once the project was established and the trial of materials in the schools begun that accounted for the changes in the project organization. As specialization became essential and the work load on each team member increased, the proposed decentralized matrix organization shown in Figure 2 became untenable. In the face of mounting pressure the only solution open to the project team was to concentrate more and more of its energies at Keele. A considerable amount of its time was still spent in the trial schools. But the flow of information became more and more one way. This was due partly to the centralization of the project at Keele and partly to the inability of the teachers to feed back information. The project team tried to maintain a decentralized, grassroots innovation. But the pressures on it and the pressures on the teachers added up to a need to centralize in order to get the work

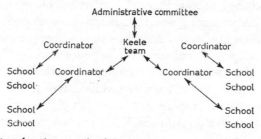

Figure 4 *Actual project organization 1970.*

done in time. In contrast to many other curriculum projects this remained localized and very closely in touch with the teachers. But it had still to give more than receive. In the end its structure was similar to that adopted by most national curriculum projects. Yet it started with probably the closest local ties of any Schools Council project.

The changes in the organization can be seen by comparing Figure 4 above with the proposed structure in Figure 2 on p. 23. This is partly the result of the failure to establish a teachers' centre. But this failure is itself a symptom of a more basic difficulty in promoting innovation in the schools rather than inserting it. As teachers found innovation exhausting, the project team, its members increasingly rushed, took more initiative to get the job finished on time. Most projects start with a centralized organization. Here the intention was to use grassroots initiative. But the context of contemporary teaching and of curriculum development combined to frustrate this intention. Local initiatives take a lot of time, central initiatives often seem irrelevant at the local level. This is the Catch 22 of curriculum development.

The role of the curriculum developer

The pressures on members of curriculum teams who are planning, introducing and helping to implement changes in schools has to be seen within the context of a school system that up to now has not included change agents. Planned curriculum innovation is in its infancy. This pioneering aspect of curriculum development accounts not only for some of the difficulties in promoting effective curriculum development, but some of the personal difficulties of those involved. There is no career structure in research and development within education. Those who are involved have to take the risk of leaving a clear-cut future to enter a job that gives every appearance of being a dead-end.[5] In the Keele project, one team member came from a university and the remaining five from school teaching. All were rather reluctant recruits to the project team.[6] All except one, a teacher who moved into a university at the end of the project, went back to their old jobs. But even within months of the end of the project all were uncertain about their future. For three years they had worked within a field divorced from established career paths. All felt that their years of working on the project had given them a unique experience and expertise in an important field. This experience would not be wasted once they returned to school. But, given the few people with experience in this field, it was wasteful that they could not have remained part of an established regional organization designed to support and sustain innovations once the trial was over.

The lack of any established career path within curriculum development was a source of anxiety for the project team, increasing as the end approached, as the amount of work increased and as future jobs became a common concern. Relations within the team were strained as involvement in the project seemed to be bringing unequal rewards. This strain was increased as the sponsors of the project, who were also those who could offer jobs, seemed to lose interest. The team experienced a sense of personal insecurity at the start of the project and met it again at the end. Given the short time span, the secure and productive middle period had been very short. But this was only one symptom of a wider problem.

The plight of the curriculum developer as marginal man has been investigated by Jenkins (1972 and in his chapter in this book). The crucial point about this marginality is that the curriculum developer is involved with the school, the university, the local education authority, and the Schools Council, but must operate in the face of their differing definitions of the situation. His own actions must take account of these different definitions. He has to develop a style of operation that enables him not only to appear credible to each of the organizations involved, but to reconcile their different demands.

The coordinators in the Keele project were in a particularly difficult position. Three were seconded by their local authorities. One was appointed by an authority from outside. All had a double allegiance.[7] They were paid by the authority but worked within the project team. Their main job was to promote the development of integrated studies in the trial schools within their area, but they were also engaged in planning the innovation at Keele.

The development of the coordinator's role came with the centralization of the organization of the project. Early in 1967 their responsibilities were listed as follows in a paper for the committee organizing the project:

The duties of coordinators, under the direction of the Director of the Humanities Project, will include:
a) Collection of data concerning the provision of courses in humanities subjects in secondary schools in the area.
b) Assistance with evaluation of data collected from within and outside.
c) Assistance in devising improvements to existing materials and procedure in this area.

d) Arranging for the testing of possible improvements.
e) Submission of periodic reports on work done.
f) Contribution to the final report of the Humanities Project.

Readers will recall that at this stage the title was still the Humanities Project. The coordinators were seen as collectors and evaluators but not as producers of curriculum packs. This was in line with other plans, which also omitted mention of material production. Yet the coordinators were to play a full part in writing curriculum packs and actually produced the first units for publication.

As the role of the coordinators was developed, so did their professional skill. But they remained uneasily poised between schools and university. They wryly commented on not being accepted as members of the university while simultaneously being treated as outsiders by the teachers in the schools. Inevitably as the project neared its end this became confused with the anxiety over future careers. They had spent three years floating in the spaces between the organizations involved, without being members of any one of them. Now they had to face the prospect of going back into the schools. The comments on this chapter by those involved give some ideas of the personal strain.

There were obviously differing solutions to this problem of marginality. As the work of the project at Keele increased, the need to obtain information on the trial in the schools simultaneously diminished. At the start of the project support had to be given and feedback had to be obtained, but this became less important in the second year of trial, and this was just the time when there was the maximum work to be done at the centre. Adopting the centralized role did not mean neglecting the schools. All the coordinators had to split their attention between their work in schools and their work at Keele. But it was possible to reduce the time spent in the schools in order to play more part in the planning of the exercise at the centre.

All field workers feel these conflicting pressures. Participant observers and anthropologists, once they get into the community being studied, tend to feel that their professional knowledge is in-adequate and their detached attitude unethical. Sometimes these pressures force them to become involved in the community beyond the point where they can remain professionally detached. In extreme cases they go native, committing themselves fully to living as one of the group, letting their links with the research project diminish and using their grant to finance an easy life under the palms with those they set out to observe.

The Keele coordinators started in an equivocal position. They seemed to have two masters – the local authorities and the project in the university. Once the pressures to concentrate energy at the centre built up and the division of labour involved them in tasks at the university, they were under strain. This was eased as the project neared its end and local authority interest waned. Consequently there was muttering on the advisory committee about the little time being spent in schools, but this was a general criticism and was not accompanied by any serious attempt to intervene by the local advisory staff.

In practice the school-based work of the coordinators was blended well with the work they did at Keele. The democratic style of organization of this project team facilitated the development of a division of labour that suited those involved. One coordinator adopted a local role, coming to Keele only when there were important team meetings.[8] Another took a more central position in the organization of the work, particularly in the accumulation of resources. The remaining two split their attention, achieving a balance. This was not a matter of personal choice alone. Nor was distance of the local authority trial schools from Keele an important factor. All the skills of this small team were needed. A lot of work was accepted and as the initial tasks of collecting examples of work in schools, of mobilizing trial schools and of getting the innovation started were completed, it was possible to spare time for jobs at the centre.

The experience of the coordinators may be a pointer to the way to overcome many of the problems of curriculum development raised in this book. They were probably the first change agents to be used, although the term was not in use when the directors of the Keele Institute thought up this type of organization. There are two sources for this optimistic view. First there was the overwhelming approval of the work of the coordinators by the teachers in the schools. This was partly because the coordinators were known as local teachers. Here was one enthusiastic teacher, answering a question on the role of the coordinators:

> I've nothing but praise. If we asked for something we got it. If something went wrong we got a visit quickly. And there was always someone to talk it all over with. I suppose it made us feel wanted.

There were criticisms. The coordinators were sometimes accused of being above the battle. There were even suggestions that they were too inexperienced to help. But this line of criticism was not destructive. 'We told him more than he told us' might have been a comment on the lack of experience of a coordinator in integrated studies, but was also a recognition that it was good to have someone from the rear to whom you could complain or boast. The teachers were also perceptive about the strain in the role of the coordinators. Here is one teacher whose main concern was the gap between the university-based project and the schools:

> He was an admin man, a resource organizer, and launched ideas. He seemed unsure as to whether he was supposed to inspire and lead or just provide. He did the latter well, but the former not at all. We didn't need ideas but the contact showed the benefits one could get from a fertile mind, conversant with the situation and experiments in other schools.

Most teachers answered this question on the coordinators by saying that it must have been difficult for them but it was a very good idea. The teachers seemed convinced that the momentum of the trial had been sustained by the links established between Keele and the schools by these locally based coordinators.

The other source of optimism lay in the way these seconded teachers rapidly adapted to the role of curriculum developers and change agents. Thirty-eight project team meetings of half a day or more were observed once a week over a period of two years. Across that time these teachers not only picked up the skills in establishing social relations within a large number of schools, not only became practised at addressing meetings and guiding other teachers, not only got used to writing curriculum materials for publication, but rapidly picked up insights into the problems that they faced. Few of the insights in this book are original or traceable to the socio-logical approach used. They come primarily from the perception of the project team as it faced new problems and reported its ex-periences.

This may be an important pointer to the way grassroots curri-culum projects could be organized. The coordinators were able to interpret the views of the project team to the teachers in a way that was readily understood. In 1969 this interpretation was done in-tuitively. By 1971 this early intuition had been disciplined into a professional approach that could detect, anticipate and solve problems as they arose. This ability to see the source and context of problems was in striking contrast to the teachers in the schools.[9] The co-ordinators had to refer problems to a range of schools, to local authority policies, to Schools Council pressures, to the recom-mendations of an advisory committee, to the requests of publishers, and to many other pressures. Their horizons had been widened and their frame of reference extended. Yet this had been done quickly and without any training programme. It was the local horizons and narrow terms of reference of the teachers that formed the main barrier to genuine implementation. The clue to successful innova-tion may lie not so much in in-service training, but in the second-ment of teachers to research and curriculum development teams. The involvement must be genuine. It was in taking responsibility for the solution of problems faced by other teachers that the coordinators came to realize the social, political and economic pressures that lie under the resistance to innovation in the schools. [10]

Bolam (1973) has illustrated the work of his team, shown in Figure 5. Here his internal view coincides exactly with my own view from the outside.

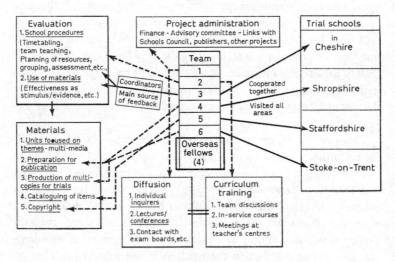

Figure 5 *The work load of team members*

1. A wide range of tasks needed to be undertaken by the project team, all focused on the central concern to understand integrated studies. The production of materials and the forming of a close working relationship with trial schools occupied members heavily from the start. Evaluation and diffusion were seen as of central importance, but the project had insufficient money and manpower for them. Curriculum training could be regarded as a basic dimension of diffusion.

2. Faced with such a range of tasks the team could have decided either to specialize heavily or for each member to take a share of each of them. In practice the latter rather than the former was agreed on. In looking at the diagram, it must be understood that every member of the team made a contribution to each of the five main aspects. In addition:

(a) *Each of the four coordinators had a personal responsibility for the trial shools in his or her LEA (shown on the diagram by a thick, unbroken line).*

(b) *Different team members took on extra jobs, some quite specific, some more generally for an aspect of the project's work (shown by a broken line).*

Such working arrangements grew up slowly and were broadly successful, but one cannot deny that the range of demands put a considerable personal strain on the coordinators, and that additional team members with specialized training (say, in evaluation) would have been highly desirable.

3. In addition to the six permanent members, the team was joined at different times by four overseas fellows, supported by either the Overseas Development Administration or UNESCO, on one-year secondments. They came from Ghana, Nigeria and Kenya. They worked as full members of the team and took part in materials production. Their presence was a stimulus to a number of discussions on contrasting problems of educational change, which widened the viewpoint of the team. Essentially their time with the project can be seen as basic training for them in curriculum development, and they have nearly all returned to key posts in such work. The whole scheme points to an extremely fruitful extension of the partnership involved in projects.

◆◆ Comments by D. R. Jenkins and Alan Townsend

[1] In spite of the difficulties and early uncertainties, possibly more national exposure at an earlier stage in the project's life would have assisted with later diffusion. Stenhouse, with his greater manpower, clear national project status and personal style, invested more heavily in promoting his ideas and materials from a fairly early stage in the life of the project. [A. T.]

[2] The overseas fellows proved very rewarding personally and socially, but they were each appointed for relatively short periods of time given the length of the project. The ways in which un-initiated new people could fit into the project varied over time. There was also in each case some degree of educational 'culture shock'. In general the project could offer over its own lifetime only a diminishing role for overseas fellows. [D. J.]

[3] The problem of catering, not for the remedial but for the below average reader above the remedial level, a problem with any materials-producing project that spans the full ability range, is, on reflection, one that merited more effort and more organized teacher involvement and inter-school sharing. In fact this was a problem that was pushed to one side, partly by the demands of the publishing timetable, although ironically at a later stage in the editing of material it became one of the issues that worried the publishers. Earlier involvement of the publishers' graphics and layout or design people and professionally produced materials at the trial stage would have been a valuable help. However, economics and other difficulties of early involvement of a publisher made this impossible (see also Chapter 8 by Bolam, pp. 165–6). [A. T.]

[4] In the case of myself and Geoff Hartley the remaining editorial work continued until March 1972, two whole terms after the end of the project. This represented a significant load to carry alongside a new job, particularly since the new job involved 'learning' the teaching role again and in career terms making a mark fairly quickly. Marginal man retreats/returns from the area of marginality. On top of this a fairly heavy load of diffusion conferences and meetings had to be carried throughout the year. Fortunately, in my case, my head, colleagues and local education authority were sympathetic and very helpful. [A. T.]

[5] My own recollection is also that there was a brittle period towards the end of the project. Some of the repressed resentments were given unaccustomed air. At a diffusion conference in the University of Sussex I found myself in dispute with Hartley and Townsend. Put in a nutshell, they felt they had been 'rowing in the middle of the boat'. In the 'musical chairs' of curriculum development they were getting the uncomfortable feeling that they would be in some way left out when somebody took the needle off the record. In addition, I was defined as a 'career opportunist', one who had

'worked his passage' on a theoretical bandwagon, and now seemed likely to use the project as a springboard to university teaching. [D. J.]

[6] Not so. The single exception was David Bolam. [D. J.]

[7] The problem of joining a short duration project is that loyalty and commitment to the ideas and the work involved in sustaining them may be strained when concern and doubts about one's own uncertain future loom ahead. In my case involvement in the publication operation helped to sustain this commitment. [A. T.]

[8] At one point the coordinator adopting a 'local' position refused to attend team meetings. This was explained in terms of prestige, which was recognized as conceded by trial schools but suspected as withheld by the trial team. In contrast, the coordinator adopting a 'central' role went to extreme lengths to maintain it, refusing the local authority office accommodation (see also Chapter 8 by Bolam, p. 142). [D. J.]

[9] The coordinators appeared to sense this. At the team meeting to discuss the diffusion conferences there were arguments against the 'over-use of trial teachers' on the grounds that 'it could be dangerous'. 'Teachers give too many details, do not see issues.' Even those whose historical role had been to pay lip-service to the notion of the practising teacher agreed: 'The trouble is that we have no control over what teachers say.' [D. J.]

[10] This tribute to the work of the coordinators appears to me to be thoroughly deserved. Feedback reports were increasingly organized around issues, and over time developed an authentic feel. This was partly a question of their becoming more perceptive and sophisticated in a complex problem area, partly a tribute to team style, which Bolam kept open and exploratory. One wonders

whether letting the coordinators drift back into what were, at least initially, classroom jobs is the best way to use their acquired wider perspectives and sharpness. And to say this is not to denigrate teaching. [D. J.]

5. The teachers' part in innovation

Pressures on the innovating teachers

The most pressing source of stress on the teachers was found in the time and energy expended. This expenditure was caused partly by the nature of integrated work, partly by the need for team planning, and partly by the demands made on teachers by active enquiry methods. But the drain on the teachers also came from the involvement in innovation itself. The part had to be learned, then played under public scrutiny. The following were quoted by teachers as sources of demands on their time and energy:

1 Preparing new materials for the new courses.
2 Rewriting Keele pack material particularly for less able children.
3 Duplicating materials for use by individual children.

1 to 3 were the consequences of a project that invited the participating teachers to develop their own approaches and materials. But some of the rewriting was necessitated by the level at which the given material was written. Aiming to cover children over a wide range of ability, it proved to be too difficult for children at the lower

end of the ability range. The materials always seemed more suitable for older or more able children than those for whom they had been designed. The observers' panel report of 1971 found the materials exactly right for grammar schools. Senior packs for schools were found suitable for further education colleges. This is a universal problem where there is a dependence on written materials, and it exercised the Keele project team throughout. It was partly the difficulty over copyright that stopped simplification of extracts and partly the result of trying to cover too broad an ability range with the limited materials. Above all, it was the common difficulty of producing written matter for children who were often barely literate.

The difficulty of using materials was increased by the way schools, without pressure from the project team, organized integrated studies in mixed ability groups. It was further exacerbated by the frequent inclusion of remedial groups against the general advice of the project team. Few of the teachers had experience of working with mixed ability groups and this increased the complexity and the vulnerability of the innovation to enquiry-based methods. There is also a tendency to over-estimate the ability and interest of children. The coordinators, after returning to teaching at the end of the project, confirmed that even after a short period out of the classroom they had forgotten how difficult many children found the simplest work and how reluctant most were to do it.

The burden of the teachers was further increased by the inclusion of a local study to be organized by the teachers. This meant additional preparation. In all this work the teachers received little help. They paid tribute to school secretaries who fitted in help between routine jobs and to county librarians who helped find sources for materials, but it was mostly do-it-yourself.

4 Arranging for multi-media use.
5 Arranging timetables.
6 Arranging rooms for enquiry methods.
7 Team meetings.

The teachers were faced with the organization of enquiry-based integrated studies using team teaching in schools where most work remained traditional. It was not just difficult to find the right sized spaces for teaching whole year groups instead of individual classes. Individual and small group work demanded a series of different sized spaces in schools that had been designed for one teacher with one class in one room.

However, even if spaces could be found, they still had to be booked in the face of opposition from other classes. But this time-tabling was complicated by the needs of team teaching. Every effort was made by the project team to get an assurance that blocks of time would be made available in place of the conventional forty-minute period. In only three of the thirty-eight schools the time-table was not blocked, and two of these left the trial at the end of the first year. In twenty-two of the thirty-eight schools the timetable was blocked specially for the Keele project.

Having obtained rooms and sufficient time, the innovators then had to obtain the necessary hardware to show slides, strips and films in rooms that could be blacked out. In many cases the school hall had to be used in competition, not only with music, games and drama, but in the face of preparations for, or cleaning up after, school dinners.

In eleven of the thirty-eight schools team meetings were scheduled within timetabled hours. In another twenty-three schools meetings were held in coffee or lunch breaks or after school. It is difficult to over-estimate the importance of these team meetings. The discussion of content and organization by different subject specialists was possibly the most stimulating part of the innovation to the visitor. But in the majority of schools it meant sacrificing free time. This was not necessarily lack of effort to provide planning time within school hours. In small schools it was impossible to release a team of six or more teachers simultaneously for a planning meeting.

The consequence was that this group of teachers were having to stay after school beyond the time when their colleagues had departed and were having to return to school in vacation time to prepare work in integrated studies. This extra effort was itself a sign of the difficulties in organizing teachers into active participation in innovation. It proved difficult to change the organization of the schools to support teachers who were establishing integrated studies, even though the work involved in accumulating material for enquiry work, in bridging conventional subject boundaries and in establishing teaching teams was very time consuming.

    8 Feedback requirements.
    9 Meetings and conferences.
   10 Visitors.

The provision of feedback was a condition of joining the trial. Forms were prepared to help teachers report on their experience. In practice, schools rarely cooperated. In only two of the thirty-eight schools was feedback judged by the project team to have been sent regularly and promptly. In another eleven schools the total amount received was judged as negligible. Six out of the seven schools that dropped out of the trial before its completion were in this category. This failure was even more disappointing given the presence of coordinators in the schools asking for information. There seems to have been a reluctance to give information and a reluctance to ask for advice.

This failure to provide feedback frustrated the intention to involve the teachers in the development. Yet in interviews teachers were fully aware of the problems involved and at conferences to publicize the project they were capable of giving advice to others of the best ways of going about integration. Again it seemed to be the effort required in producing feedback combined with reluctance to publicize problems that stopped this active participation.

This difficulty in getting active as distinct from passive cooperation from teachers could also be detected in the frequent requests from teachers at meetings and in interviews for more guidance, more instruction on how to work integrated studies, and more model courses. Even at diffusion conferences at the end of the trial period there was an expectation among the teachers attending that a prescription was needed that could be followed, rather than guidelines within which teachers could develop their own style.

The difficulties over obtaining feedback were partly caused by the private nature of conventional classroom teaching that makes teachers reluctant to expose their problems to the public. Yet innovation inevitably increased the visibility of the innovating teachers. The project directors and coordinators were often in the schools. Inspectors, advisers, Schools Council field officers, parents, visiting speakers and observers and researchers engaged in evaluation were also frequent visitors. Each took up time. This increased the strain on the innovating teachers. But there was a threshold beyond which this public attention could deepen the commitment to innovation. In nine of the thirty-eight schools the teachers, and more particularly the headteachers, seemed to have a self-identity as leaders in an important educational development. These schools now welcomed visitors and evaluations. They derived strength from the spotlight on their work.

Attendance at conferences and meetings was another sign that a school was investing in innovation. Meetings at Keele, at local teachers' centres and between trial schools were an essential part of the organization of the project. Sixteen of the twenty-two 'successes' contained teachers who were regular attenders at meetings, while four of the seven 'failures' had teachers who were judged as rarely attending.

Attendance at meetings, visits to other trial schools and exchanges of information between the teachers involved were essential to a project aiming to mobilize active teacher participation. The difficulties encountered lay partly in the absence of teachers' centres. But even where there were facilities, teachers seemed unwilling or unable to spare the time, and meetings were poorly attended.

In retrospect more could have been done to improve communication between teachers by means of a news-sheet or simply written progress reports. The coordinators did circulate information between schools but were increasingly involved in the central organization. At meetings there was a casual exchange of information between teachers but the distances between schools, the shortage of money and the difficulties in arranging visits between schools, especially across local authority boundaries, made it difficult to carry out the original objective of establishing a local, teacher-directed project.

A variety of individual motives involved in the decision to join the innovation and in the drive to translate that innovation into a personal style, were influenced by both the conditions of conventional teaching and by the nature of the innovating role. The teachers involved here were particularly concerned with the following:

1 The need to learn new knowledge.
2 The need to become involved in new conceptual frameworks.

Although the material in the Keele project was designed to arch over such subjects as history, geography, English, religious education and art, it stretched the skills and knowledge of the teachers. First it forced specialists in one subject to learn selected aspects of others. In practice, the teachers went too far in trying to become multi-subject experts, but in team teaching children, operating across conventional subject boundaries, expected teachers to do the same. These teachers also had to introduce new work and this usually meant involving more than one discipline.

The second new area of knowledge was the social sciences. Integrated studies inevitably draws on anthropology and sociology. In the Keele project the most popular unit consisted of comparative studies of Tristan da Cunha, Dayaks in Borneo and Imperial China. None of these were liable to be in the teacher's normal repertoire. The consequent need to learn new facts was a small assignment compared with the difficulty faced by the teachers in using new concepts often derived from the social sciences.

3 Separation from class teaching.
4 Separation from subject teaching.

The feeling of deprivation among teachers involved in some form of team teaching recurred in interviews, Most teachers were simultaneously involved in conventional and team teaching, but the latter made many uneasy. The flexible nature of this project made it easy for teachers to opt out of a team and return to conventional classroom teaching. Many schools deliberately change from having a fixed team at the start to a more flexible structure in which teachers could join or leave easily.

It would be wrong to over-emphasize any insecurity resulting from the move away from subject teaching. There were important cases where the subject discipline was a fundamental support for the teacher as well as being seen as crucial by him. Teachers of religious education were particularly uneasy. Integrated studies was seen as a way of introducing a broader, more comparative perspective. But these teachers of religious education tended to be the first in and the first out. They withdrew because they felt that it was impossible to ensure that basic values were transmitted in a team context and with curriculum materials that stressed the relativity of human values. Another group to express disquiet were teachers of English. Here the worry was the small amount of formal written work included in integrated studies.

It is an important belief among sociologists of education that subjects, once learned, are not readily surrendered. In learning and teaching a subject a teacher invests so much that he will defend his subject and oppose integration. But this view has little evidence to support it and here the opposite was true. The teachers were only too keen to jettison their subjects even though the project team was opposed to this. Some teachers defended the boundaries of their subject, but many were only too willing to sell the pass. The disquiet after integration was due to the difficulties of team teaching rather than to the surrender of subject frontiers.

This feeling of deprivation from a secure classroom arose from involvement with what was basically a larger group of children. While individual and small group work occurred, individual teachers were still concerned with a whole year group of around 150

children in a variety of rooms, rather than a class of thirty confined
with them in the same classroom. The teachers felt that they did not
get to know the children as well. They stressed that there were
advantages for the children in the mixing that occurred, but for
them it had not the same quality of contact.

This feeling was related to the strain of innovation. Team teaching and inquiry methods involved teachers in work with individuals or small groups. Information had to be given tailor-made, not
in a standard packet to a whole school class. The teachers expressed
this as giving information a hundred times to individuals rather than
to classes of thirty at a time. These were secondary school teachers,
trained to conventional techniques. The adjustment to new methods
was difficult.

    5 Anxiety about standards.
    6 Difficulties in evaluating integrated work.

Most teachers were concerned in case there had been a drop in
standards. They were still subject specialists who feared that the
children would not learn the essential skills of the subject disciplines.
There seemed to be agreement that there had been a drop in standards at the start of the trial period. This was seen as compensated
by the increased activity of the children and by the gains from being
able to involve a variety of subjects in the study of the same topic.

The concern over the apparent temporary drop in standards was
increased by difficulties over the way integrated studies could be
assessed. Banks of questions were prepared by the project team to
help teachers. However, the traditional use of tests, essays and
examinations was inappropriate when the product of the integrated
work might have been a skill in finding out, an exhibition arranged
by a group of children, or a tape recording. Work could no longer
be assessed as the learning of facts by individuals. The report of the
observers' panel stressed that assessment was the greatest single
problem presented to teachers by the project. Here are teachers describing the difficulties:

Assessment and evaluation is probably the most difficult aspect of integrated work where extensive use of individual and group work is used. Teachers found it more difficult to write out terminal reports and assess attainment and progress.

Gave us much heart-searching on question of whether course had failed or succeeded – how could we assess progress, therefore how could we measure any success of course? When we finally came to grips with assessment and experiment with it we achieved something. So course succeeded in making us come to grips with a very important educational issue.

These were typical responses. The worry over standards and assessment also centred on external examinations. By 1971 arrangements for CSE examinations had been made. Integrated studies was to count as two subjects, thus removing the fear that the integration of subjects would mean a loss in the number of subjects in which passes could be obtained. This concern was coupled with the worry over the possibility that standards would, at least initially, fall after integration. English teachers were concerned about basic literary skills. Geographers worried that basic techniques would be overlooked. Teachers of religious education were anxious about the absence of a clear Christian message.

It was this combination of anxiety over the threat to subject skills and difficulties over assessment that accounted for the early withdrawal of schools from the trial. With experience both problems were solved. In interviews after the end of the trial period the positive side of this concern emerged. To the project team, concern over assessment often seemed excessive, but it was a genuine worry about the attainment of children. This was not limited to standards of work. Teachers often said that they had detected insecurity among the children, just as they had felt insecure once the insulation in their own classrooms had gone. Here is a teacher's view of the insecurity of children in a team teaching, enquiry-based learning situation:

D

Children enjoyed and were stimulated by course but were anxious about missing conventional lessons. They seem to like the security of a 'framework' they can understand and were too immature to understand the value to them of a more complex approach.

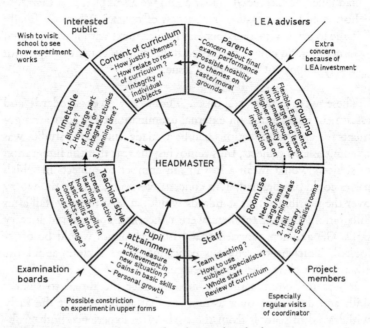

Figure 6 *The impact of integrated studies on the school*

Any school is a 'combined operation', but any curriculum change – let alone one as complex as integrated studies – will disturb its equilibrium and move it towards a new pattern of interrelationships.

The headmaster is seen as the focus of all changes in school life, without any suggestion that they all originate in him. Aspects which are seen to have a close connection with each other are placed opposite, though the nature of the link may vary; the fact, for example, that parents have a very strong concern for the attainment of their children is clearly a different kind of interrelationship than that between timetabling and room use. Nor can such links be regarded as exclusive.

This was a typical remark, showing the shrewd way that teachers analysed the impact of the innovation. Bolam (1973) has illustrated the problems facing schools introducing integrated studies in Figure 6. My only disagreement is that the diagram exaggerates the importance of the headteacher in many schools. The head's role could be central, but he could also be only vaguely aware that something new was going on in his school.

Successful and unsuccessful innovators

The ideal teacher for the Integrated Studies Project was one willing to maintain his subject discipline within a team and to engage in planning integrated work through discussions with other specialist colleagues. This teacher would be an active producer of new materials, teaching methods and ideas for integrated subject work. He would keep accounts of his innovatory work, fill in the questionnaires and schedules sent from Keele and feed his experience back to the project team. He would organize his work so that children would not only come to see and use the concepts within separate subject disciplines, but would learn the skills of those subjects through enquiry-based programmes.

In practice this ideal was rarely realized. The teachers were mainly concerned with the immediate problems facing them in the classroom. They were grateful for the ideas and the materials, and often were convinced that integrated studies was both educationally desirable and liable to motivate children more than traditional subject teaching. But their main concern was with concrete problems of discipline and the maintenance and assessment of standards of work. Principles of integration, the niceties of team teaching, and the commitment to feed back experiences to the project were often ignored.

Actual measures of the success of the project in the schools are given in Chapter 7. In three schools the project was never really introduced, although the schools were officially committed to trial. In four more schools the project was only superficially implemented and did not last the first year of trial. In one more school the project continued throughout two years, but in little more than name only. It must be stressed that this fictitious or superficial implementation in schools was known to the project team. Similar proportions would be likely in other projects. New trial schools were introduced to keep the numbers up. What is of concern here is why these schools, having committed themselves to the trial, did little more than take project materials and leave them in a cupboard.

Press-ganging

The investigation of the schools that dropped out in the first year showed that three had headteachers who had been enthusiastic supporters for the introduction of integrated studies, but where this enthusiasm was not shared by the teachers. Of the thirty-eight schools involved between 1969 and 1971 eight had teachers who seemed to have been pressed into the project. Five of these completed the trial. However, three experienced the lowest amount of curriculum change, the least degree of change in attitude towards integrated studies and little change in school organization. But press-ganging did not always lead to rapid drop-out or to the failure of the innovation. In two of these schools there was not only successful completion of the trial but a high level of curriculum change after the end of the trial period. Both had started with no signs of experiments in the integrated direction, but ended by rearranging their curriculum and organization to facilitate further integration.

This success by press-ganged teachers could be contrasted with the failure in other schools where the staff had been enthusiastic volunteers. This indicates the shallow nature of this analysis and the dangers of generalization. An authoritarian head could inhibit or inspire a team. A democratic head could promote initiative or inertia. Some schools seemed to fizz with ideas while others stagnated. A part of Halpin's Organizational Climate Description Questionnaire (1966) was used to detect this esprit. But this served only to confirm subjective impressions, not to explain the factors that were involved.

There were also two schools where, at the end of the project, a new head was appointed who stopped integrated studies despite the wish of the teaching team to continue. To an outsider this seemed even more arbitrary than pressing teachers into the project. It meant that in ten of thirty-eight schools there seemed to have been no consultation before a decision was made by the head. But this was the teachers' view. The heads concerned were convinced that there had been consultation. It may have been a wish of the teachers to give the visiting researcher a good reason for giving up the work. It was more likely to have been a difference in the definition of the school situation between heads and teachers. A head's consultation might seem dictation to the teachers.

There was one other possible explanation for the apparently arbitrary decisions of heads. Throughout the project the teachers simultaneously asked for a clear blueprint to follow and freedom to adjust materials and methods to their own classroom conditions. At the diffusion conferences at Keele and Brighton in 1971, there was a similar demand for apparently conflicting procedures. The project was criticized for not presenting a complete course for action, yet the units it did present were criticized as too restricting. The answer may be in the lack of opportunity for teachers to join in decision-making, their consequent reluctance to engage in consultation and their defence against criticisms of this stance based on their main area of authority, concern and expertise in their class-rooms. Thus heads, like curriculum planners, may have no other option than making apparently arbitrary decisions. The fault may lie in the closed nature of teaching in schools.

The rewards of innovation

The interviews with the teachers who had been involved revealed a wide spectrum of interests and attitudes. At one extreme were teachers who had taken little trouble to understand what the project was all about. They confessed to never having read documents that were sent to them, never attended conferences and paid little attention to the advice of the coordinators. At the other extreme were teachers who not only used the materials offered by the project, but added to them out of their own efforts, fed back their experiences with these materials, reorganized their methods of teaching, attended conferences and vigorously debated the principles behind the introduction of integrated studies. These teachers were not necessarily in the schools on which the project had the maximum impact. They could be very critical. They were not in amenable trial schools giving first priority to trying out the ideas of the project. They were probably more effective as teachers, but often appeared as obstructive to the project team. This is once again a difficulty for Schools Council projects. The Schools Council (Banks 1969, Caston 1971) saw the responsibilities of trial schools in the relevant areas of work as being primarily to the project. But these teachers, who were the most concerned, and often the hardest working, were just those who were liable to press on with their own local ideas. Many of these teachers contributed new materials and ideas to the project. They made it their project, pressed on with their ideas and in this sense frustrated the trial.

It was these energetic teachers who illustrated the difficulties of talking about an innovatory teaching role. The introduction of integrated studies often served as a catalyst, enabling these teachers to speed up changes in their schools. They were defining and redefining their role. They were doing this within the context of their schools. The project was only one part of their work. It was helping them to overcome only one of their problems. When these teachers were asked to assess the impact of the experience of being engaged in a project, they could not sort out the various influences upon them. The project acted as the stimulus to set or keep them going, but the direction in which they went was determined by many other pressures. The Keele project encouraged this variety, and diversity of response was welcomed. But it would have frustrated many other curriculum development projects.

The pressures faced by these innovating teachers and the responses to them suggest that there are two important characteristics of the work of teachers that must be taken into account if they are to play a part in developing curriculum in their schools. The first concerns the extra work involved. Teachers may, or may not, be overworked. But what clearly emerges from this study is that those teachers who were involved in innovating within the school felt that they were overworked compared with other teachers. This did not only apply to their work within the project. In interviews they maintained that they were also the teachers to run extra-curricular activities. Curiously the headteachers interviewed tended to confirm this view. They admitted they did call upon these active teachers to to the various extra jobs around the school. The principle seemed to be that 'if you want something done, ask a busy man or woman'. Here the importance of rewards becomes apparent. These teachers felt that they were taking the strain while other teachers were carrying on with the easy life. 'What do we get out of it?' was a repeated question.

The answer to this question of rewards is partly material. But these teachers were also the ones who were probably most concerned with the education of the children in their care. This was their reason for enthusiastically innovating. It lies behind their concern with the effects of innovation on standards of work. This is often expressed as a fear that examination results will get worse. This may seem narrow minded but it was part of the concern that these teachers felt. The project in this sense was a potential threat while simultaneously offering hopes of improvement, particularly for less able children. There was therefore some intrinsic reward in innovation, once the teachers could be assured that the work of the pupils would not suffer. But there were also rewards in the contact with outsiders that innovation can bring. If the source of complaint lay in comparisons with other teachers in the same school, the sources of rewards often lay in contact with outsiders coming into the school to see how innovation was going. In some cases, described later as 'limelight' schools, this seemed to affect a majority of the teachers. But in other cases individual teachers came to value the contact with coordinators, advisers, visiting students, researchers and so on. The interviewing of these teachers was a rare pleasure. They wanted to tell someone about their work. It may be that one of the weaknesses of the present structure of schooling is that teachers are isolated from the public recognition of their work. Much of the pain and pleasure of teaching is within a closed class-room. Team teaching can open this up and any innovation can serve to bring teachers into the limelight. Once this happens the sources of reward outside the school may be strong enough to overcome the depression that occurs through comparisons with other '9 to 4' teachers.

The Keele project had the advantages of being local, of asking the teachers to help in the development of curriculum materials, and of employing coordinators. But it has already been argued that the project team was marginal to the university in which it operated and to the schools in which the project was implemented. This limited the reward that teachers could derive from the project team. The coordinators were usually local teachers, valuable for their intimate knowledge of local problems, but lacking the prestige that attaches to academics in colleges and universities. In some cases the project team was seen to be getting recognition while asking the teachers to do the work. 'What are we getting out of it?' was placed alongside 'What are they getting out of it?' The reluctance to feed back information could have been related to this feeling. But the severest criticism was reserved in the interviews for what the teachers felt was academic condescension. Some of this has been referred to in the teachers' responses to early documents on the principles of integration. It was an attitude of 'How can you tell how I have to teach?' or 'How can they have any idea of how I have to implement their ideas?' Yet these were responses to a local, open-ended project organized to have close links with schools. The harshest criticism of all was reserved in references to other projects where staff headquarters were far away from the battleground. Here the teachers felt that they were offered irrelevant, idealistic advice, with no chance of any reward in the form of recognition and not even the thanks of the organizers.

One benefit of the local nature of the project was that the ideas developed at Keele could be tried out in the classroom. Hartley, a coordinator, comments:

> Team members did on occasions, although much too rarely, join trial school teams and actually teach their own material. A sobering experience.
>
> However, given more time, it would have been an excellent idea for the whole project team to form a sort of 'commando unit' to operate in a school for, say, half a term. I feel that this would have greatly helped relations with schools, would have been an excellent trial of materials, and would have provided a wealth of general feedback.

The Keele project was compared favourably by the trial school teachers when they were asked about other curriculum projects. There is a distance between teachers and other parts of the education system that may inhibit innovation. Early talks with teachers showed the strength of this feeling. Its recognition accounts for the stress in the following chapter on the relation between inputs and outputs and the role of rewards for the teachers involved. At its extreme it was expressed as a feeling that they were on a 'hiding to nothing' once they came into contact with researchers or developers. For the majority it was a feeling that they were being used but not recognized. They felt that they were often on the receiving end of advice that was irrelevant, and were never asked for their own experiences, which to them were the genuinely valid ones. This criticism was rarely aimed directly at the Integrated Studies Project. The teachers expressed surprise that the project asked for advice rather than gave it. Sometimes this seemed to them a weakness in the project design. But the interviews were taken as the opportunity to point out to at least one university lecturer why teachers often seem obstinate. They knew that I would benefit from doing the research. They also knew that all they were likely to get was criticism in my final report.

David Jenkins

6. Schools, teachers and curriculum change

Chapter 3 has already looked at the way in which the various agents involved in the Integrated Studies Project defined their work. This chapter is an attempt to extend that analysis. The purpose of the attempt is to draw attention to a range of issues that would repay closer attention if we hope to understand the process of curriculum innovation itself. The interpretative description offered here is very much the viewpoint of a single observer, but tape-recorded interviews with over forty teachers allow a wealth of illustration to fill out the analysis. Illustration, of course, falls some way short of demonstration. The reader is therefore invited to judge the plausibility of the account for himself.

So what is the problem? Simply that the relationship between the Keele project and its trial teachers was characterized by a number of ambiguities. Not only was there a sense in which the teachers had a viewpoint that could be distinguished from the viewpoints held by other agencies in the endeavour – the local authority, the project team, the Institute of Education and the Schools Council – but also there was wide disagreement among the teachers themselves. This was not merely that different teachers adjudicated differently the problems posed by the project; it was rather that there were widely differing interpretations about the nature of the exercise, and the 'contractual obligation', if any, that existed towards Keele.

Part of this ambiguity springs from the nature of curriculum development as it has been institutionalized through Schools Council curriculum development projects, and part from the peculiar features of 'integrated humanities'. The Schools Council itself walks a tightrope on the one hand, its very existence appearing to assert that the 'secret garden' of the curriculum must be more publicly accountable for its horticultural practices – in short that the curriculum is a legitimate object of social policy. On the other hand, the Schools Council is constitutionally protected from becoming an agent of DES policy-making. It is 'an independent body with a majority of teacher members'. Its purpose is to 'undertake' in England and Wales research and development work in curricula, teaching methods and examinations in schools. This is subject to the 'general principle' that each school should 'have the fullest measure of responsibility for its own work'. Schools concentrating their attention on the notion of development could be forgiven for supposing that curriculum projects are merely supportive agencies for school-based curriculum growth. In practice, however, projects tend to be set up within what is a watered-down version of a research paradigm. There may not be overt insistence on control groups and comparative testing, but there is at least the assumption that a single product is being tested, perhaps in a manner akin to consumer research. According to this view a project cannot totally disperse its identity by allowing an infinite reinterpretation. One teacher saw both the project and its trial schools as groping for a style. The central commitment was to this evolving style, but any individual school would be engaged in ongoing local reinterpretation.

This dilemma is heightened in the case of a project looking at the problems and possibilities of an integrated approach to humanities teaching. Nobody supposes that this is an area in which an imposed curriculum scheme would be appropriate. There is also some uncertainty about what is to count as integration, particularly as the Keele project flirted with a number of models or alternative possibilities. Equally, although the Keele project took an exceptionally wide view of the humanities area of the curriculum (as any theme, topic, or problem-based work drawing on the range of disciplines offering rational or imaginative insight into the human condition) in any individual school, staffing and other exigencies were always likely to result in an amalgamation of teachers or subjects that imperfectly reflected this abstract overview of what could be involved. Thus some schools involved the social sciences or the creative arts, but others did not. One school had eight teachers involved, another had only one. The simplest possible question that could be asked of any curriculum project, 'Precisely what is it that you are recommending?' was in this instance not likely to draw forth a simple or straightforward answer. An earlier document put the point slightly differently:

> Our first problem, then, is purely descriptive. It goes in that saying that the school curriculum cannot avoid being broken down into organizing categories whether they are called 'subject', 'theories', 'topics' or 'problems'. Integrated studies as an idea depends upon the selection of organizing categories that are themselves supra-subject. A school approaching a theme like Masks will need to relate several 'subjects' or styles of enquiry. Having said this, however, it soon becomes clear that integrated studies is a widely sheltering umbrella. For example, a school's commitment to an integrated approach could be 'limited' or 'extended', both in terms of time and complexity of collaboration. Although the project has offered most support to schools accepting both a long-range commitment and a high degree of professional collaboration, it must not be thought that either of these features are formally necessary to integrated studies. It is important to realize that 'limited' and 'extended' commitment may predispose schools towards different styles of characterizing their units. 'Limited' schools may talk of 'bridging opportunities' from existing subjects, 'extended' schools may describe themselves, ambiguously, as breaking down subject barriers.

It has already been made clear that the Keele project was organized in a way that broke clear from the traditional centre-peripheral model of institutionalized curriculum development. The typical project, in spite of the Schools Council espousal of the imagery of a grassroots curriculum movement, is set up within a development and implementation model in which the project team is 'central' and the trial schools 'peripheral'. This model has overtones of a classical tradition, as though the purpose of the exercise were to civilize the outposts. The Keele project accepted, even welcomed, the modification of its material, and took the view that the conditions of trial were open to negotiation and transaction. By appointing full-time coordinators in each of the local authority areas, the Keele project openly acknowledged the need for link men versed in the perspectives both of the project trial schools and of the Institute of Education. Their marginal status certainly created problems, some of which have been explored earlier, but the central intention was clear-cut.

In this chapter we take as problematic the definitions arrived at by trial school teachers. These definitions cover a range of 'preferred meanings' about both the school-based task of working in an integrated studies team, and also the nature of the perceived link with the development project itself. It is suggested that in curriculum innovation of the kind under study teachers find themselves in a whole series of social situations that call into question their frameworks of social comparison. The reference orientations of teachers (how they perceive themselves and those others whose views or values are significant to them) will be important here. A teacher may feel himself a member of a community of scholars specializing academically in one of the disciplines. If so he may resist a move towards integrated studies, resisting the supposedly concomitant need to redefine himself as a 'generalist'. Other individual teachers, merely by virtue of association with a university – or the very cachet of innovation itself – may perceive themselves in fact or fantasy as part of a more favoured group. Such individuals value occupational self-identification with the 'change agent' role and even entertain exaggerated ideas about the contribution that could be played by education in effecting social change in general.

A resistant group may go through a crisis in identity. In a number of schools resistant teachers have used banter aggressively as a means of degrading the innovators, not entirely in jest. Each example has in common the need felt by teachers to be anchored to a perspective that orders the distressing complexities of the new environment.

Self-evidently a curriculum project is an attempt to manipulate the reference orientations of teachers. The starting point in this interpretative account is a suggestive analogy. A sociological perspective on organ transplantation suggests that completely novel social relationships throw a peculiar strain on all participants. Organ transplantation cannot be considered simply as a problem in medical technology, as it raises issues about what appropriate social framework unites donor or next-of-kin and the recipient. Social relationships are governed by a web of reciprocity that evolves over time. The absence of cultural norms and expectations poses problems of what behaviour is 'appropriate'. The suggestion is that in the uncertainty all participants are driven back towards guiding metaphors. The donor may be seen as sacrificial victim or generous friend. He may be seen as offering himself, or disposing of what is no longer his to give. The language describing the donor's act may legitimately vary from the transcendental to the cool.

Similarly, the relationship of a curriculum project to its trial schools is a novel social relationship. The existing models (inspectorial, research-based, etc.) are all to some extent uncomfortable. How the Keele project was perceived by its trial school teachers may be best understood by analysing the guiding metaphors that were generated. The suggestion is not that these guiding metaphors were in every sense explicitly held analogies. Rather they are constructed imaginatively to allow a certain sharpness and irony in our interpretative description. Teachers are, however, prone to use such metaphors in everyday conversation. For one teacher, the project had 'shot some material into the school's arm' and was 'staying around to watch the circulation and prevent phlebitis'.

Life blood . . . or dope? The quotations are from taped interviews.
I thought it better to use these with minimal context, to adorn the
general thesis, although in some ways a school-by-school account
would have been more illuminating, not to say entertaining! The
guiding metaphors are not in any real sense mutually exclusive and
I am not claiming that the chapter is written to a tight logic. There
were probably nine major responses:

1. *The exchange of gifts:* The project as reciprocal obligation
2. *The other drummer:* The project as unselected affinity
3. *Troubled waters:* The project as agitation or distress
4. *The gift of grace:* The project as salvation
5. *New props for identity:* The project as theatre
6. *Free sample:* The project as commercialism
7. *Ground bait:* The project as exploitation
8. *Taking issue:* The project as management consultancy
9. *Cargo cult:* The project as overwhelming technology

1 The exchange of gifts: The project as reciprocal obligation

'We didn't feel guilty because, I would say, any project which
involves environmental work and which is composed at a distance
from the environment in which it is to be used is almost certainly
going to have to be amended and adapted.' (headteacher)

'I think possibly I have twinges of conscience occasionally when
I lean away from things towards my own interests, because I
appreciate, you know, that you want us to follow a brief. You
want us more or less to follow the curriculum, because otherwise
you can't judge it.' (rural teacher)

'We're not a trial school. Just helping out.' (trial school teacher)

The metaphor of the gift-exchange allows the school to see (or deny) contact with a curriculum project as an exchange of mutual tokens, or obligations. The school is showered with gifts and benefits, such as advice and curriculum material, but is implicitly expected to 'enter a contract'. The school pays back in allowing house-room to the innovation, in hospitality, feedback and general support. The emphasis is on reciprocal obligation. The Keele project coordinators became by one account 'watchdogs' on behalf of the agreement, and therefore quasi-inspectorial, at least in the 'factory inspector' sense.

Paradoxically, the more 'guilty' a school feels about not implementing the conditions of trial ('We didn't like to tell him we weren't using the stuff, he's such a nice guy') the more the curriculum project worker visiting the school may enjoy a number of fringe benefits. He will probably be offered free tea or even free school 'dinners', the latter served with appropriate ritual by the domestic science department. The social rules governing this exchange can be very complex and mystifying. One school thought to make explicit the exchange through a ritual in which the visitor's offer to pay would be graciously refused. When I left one school, having forgotten to offer, I was tracked down across three counties by a whole posse of school secretaries.

The gift exchange can either be diplomatic or friendly. 'Diplomatic' contact involved a rich fantasy life concerning what life was actually like at Keele. For one group of teachers it was an outing, a treat even, to go to the centre ('We like to go to the hub of things; its a whole day's journey but definitely worth it; and a day out of Squaresville'); another darkly mentioned hints of the good life at Keele ('idle hours at Keele spent dreaming up schemes, and punting down the river and drinking gin in the evenings'). Another teacher said that the thought of Keele, 'Up there, strange and powerful like a monster', drove her 'crazy' – it isn't only the curriculum traveller who speculates about unexplored lands. It was true also that the diplomatic visitor would be allowed on occasion a coordinating style based on the notion of an intellectual feudal system. Some of the schools that did not become trial schools complained that the project's single lordly visit was conducted in a Foreign Office manner ('I couldn't stomach that plummy accent or those cautious abstract sentences'). It is surprisingly hard for occasional visitors to schools to get past the headmaster's study.

There is at times almost a clear assumption that diplomatic contact ought to be confined to 'ambassador' level and based on the exchange of symbolic trinkets from the respective milieux, and other unearned tokens of esteem. The hint that the tokens need not be earned came in several uses of the word 'flattery' ('Well, this is in a way flattering you know, to feel that for the first time something you say has got relevance to a larger body of work', 'Being observed in a team teaching situation is so flattering that you want some kind of reassurance from time to time in turning to those concerned with the project as a whole'). When one of the coordinators offered to 'keep a fatherly eye' on an erring trial school one sensed from his tone that the phrase contained a preference for indulgence over toughness.

The diplomatic exchange has one advantage over the management consultancy metaphor. It reduces the threat of contact with an outside body, by making the relationship expressive rather than instrumental. Several teachers expressed some variation of the view that their school had become an 'outpost' of Keele. Most appropriate garb for the curriculum visitor travelling to an outpost is a lightweight tropical suit.

The alternative model for reciprocal obligation is based on friendship. The friendly neighbourhood curriculum visitor is 'really' a buddy, a practising teacher who happens to be on a temporary skive. His exchange of gifts is much more likely to be with the classroom teachers, although his identification with them may be equivocal. The Keele coordinators often adopted the stance of 'practising teachers' at team meetings, but as their own capacity for identifying wider issues grew, this hat was worn less jauntily. Equally in the schools they were not averse to pushing towards a

E

sharpened awareness of issues. They could not overplay the theory, however ('He has been really helpful; he sees things from our point of view and helps us to interpret the project'). Friendship disarms, removing the need for diplomatic immunity. The curriculum visitor bypasses the office. He gains honorary membership of in-school cliques. Banter and in-jokes become the typical medium of communication, and he is expected to over-dramatize his similarity to other teachers. Inside information and routine grouses are a part of the currency of exchange, although there is an un-written understanding that tokens are not negotiable outside the group. Most appropriate garb for the curriculum visitor is a sports jacket with real leather elbows.

2 The other drummer: The project as unselected affinity

'I hadn't realized that this was what was planned. I suppose I should have, but it wasn't made clear to me when I joined the humanities that my art time would be cut out. Later I was asked by the head of the geography department how much time I wanted to give a talk on African Art and I said one-and-a-half periods. And I prepared it with slides. It came to the end of the first period, when I was just beginning to sort of make things fit together with other slides, and he said, "I am afraid you will have to finish there." Rather off-putting, to say the least.' (art teacher)

'Well we were cautious because we had just had a highly success-ful year without Keele. . . . When we were approached in the first place we possibly had reservations inasmuch that I think if we hadn't done Keele, we would have been equally successful, possibly even more successful.' (team leader)

No teacher is an island. Teachers' ideas about teaching can be traced back to their various sources. These persist as anchoring points of proved usefulness in organizing the complexities of the environment. Some of these anchoring points may be influential individuals, others may be bodies of doctrine offering some ideological or professional perspective. Yet others may be hand-me-down formulae, practitioners' tips for survival in the world of the classroom. These 'guidelines' exist in the social world of the teacher through reference groups or reference individuals (e.g. a body like NATE, the National Association of Teachers of English, or a single charismatic headteacher). Reference-group theory, in Robert Merton's formulation, is concerned with 'those processes of evaluation and self-appraisal in which the individual takes the values and standards of others as a frame of reference' (Merton 1968). The term echoed in our section heading, 'selective affinity', was coined to describe the problems faced by persons enjoying membership of several groups. It also applies to problems of allegiance posed by the need to choose between conflicting reference groups. In such circumstances, individuals affine selectively. It was not difficult to spot that a number of trial school teachers had the kind of weakened commitment to the project that comes from 'following a different drummer'. There is, of course, nothing disreputable about this, whether or not teachers were open about what was happening. Some were; some were not. Neither would it be true to say that the better teachers were those who felt the fullest commitment. A number of really thoughtful teachers carried reservations in some areas or made personal accommodations within their own looser interpretation of the project's ideology. Equally some of the 'totally committed' teachers seemed to outside observers to be relatively clueless about the main issues to be faced by teachers of integrated studies.

In this choice between conflicting perspectives, where did opposition to the Keele project's recommendations come from? The obvious prediction, that integrated studies would call into question the nature of a teacher's affiliation to subjects or departments, proved a correct one. It did not matter whether the perceived differences in perspective were 'real' or not. The point is that they were either asserted by teachers or implicit in how they behaved. The Keele project's trial school teachers came to integrated studies from many different backgrounds. Some were graduate teachers with some personal intellectual investment in an established academic tradition ('I still see myself as a very academic English teacher; my first question is, "What is in this pack for the English teacher?" '). Others came up from the 'integrated day' in the primary school and viewed secondary integration in a child-centred way, reacting violently, for example, to epistemological arguments for integration, notions like 'key explaining concepts' or even an attempt to see subjects as instruments of exploration and enquiry. Curiosity is all, and the only 'model making' involves the use of cardboard and putty rather than more abstract modes of thought. One teacher was 'absolutely sick of putty models'. Another, who was given 'no choice' but was 'pitched in' to the integrated studies team, complained that the Keele project team had no relevant primary school experience! And this for a project working explicitly in the secondary area ('I thought that the whole idea of environmental study groups and combined studies was perhaps something more like a junior school situation . . . you know, interest-based; haven't any of you from Keele taught in a junior school?'). Another teacher, this time in a middle school, saw the project as extending the freedom of the infant school, through primary education and into the middle school. Given the resistance of the teachers to the 'theoretical bumph' handed out by Keele, it is no wonder that towards the end of the project some teachers were beginning to suspect that 'our view of integrated studies is in some ways different from Keele's'.

The issue of subject specialization is very important to teachers who have to face up to the career risks implicit in a move to integrated studies. Pervading subject ideologies could either help or hinder, again in predictable ways. The geography teacher acquainted with the thrust towards quantification in the 'new geography' could be accused of merging his subject's identity just at a time when it is striving to re-establish itself. At least two teachers found this dilemma personally painful. Similarly, English teachers were aided in their move towards integrated studies by the English-is-every-where movement that had already invaded this no-man's-land between subjects and was happily developing an anthology-around-issues approach to the teaching of literature. Indeed this is a part of the conventional wisdom of NATE. On the other hand, physical educationists brought captive within the gates of integrated studies were as likely to murmur darkly about the mystique of 'one man controlling' the gymnasium and despair of the vagaries of team teaching in a large hall (one such character was observed for a whole double period sitting moodily, legs dangling over the stage). The position of the religious education teacher was frequently (in both senses) instructive. Almost pathetically insistent on inclusion within the team, presumably hoping to exchange an open approach to religious subject-matter for the even more fashionable stance of a religious approach to open subject-matter, the religious education teacher frequently became heavily disenchanted ('I feel that the content of religious education can be got over – the same message – in integration; obviously, living in this country there should be a bias towards the Christian faith; when we did the local study we had lessons on the family and religion; but when we moved on to other communities I wondered: what on earth are we doing that is Christian here?'). It is in the nature of reference groups that they allow assertions to be made as 'obvious' by one group that would be denied by others. The project team did not have a single voice on this one. In fact, faced with the above statement, team response would have varied between approval and horror.

There were other clashes of perspective. A teacher with a diploma in social administration, finding himself in an enquiry-centred free-wheeling outfit, looked in vain either for the educational equivalent of 'management by objectives' or even a satisfactory role model among his integrated studies colleagues for his own professional development ('I've been looking for role models, but I haven't found any'). Other teachers with experience of integrated studies elsewhere (e.g. at Henbury School, Bristol) or in the same school before the project arrived, often had already established preferred ways of looking at things. There is also the small matter of prestige. One nationally known school, whose reputation was established before it joined the project, did not in its public relations activities stress or even mention the link it subsequently developed. Far from wishing to acquire the prestige of Keele, it saw itself as defending its prestige against the possible misinterpretation that its work was largely inspired by the Keele project. Different views could be taken of the actual risk involved, but the intention was unmistakable.

Other drummers too, were beating the project bounds. In one local authority, an adviser taking around a team member from another Schools Council project took the opportunity in public to offer sour comments on the Keele project. In another authority a working group on integrated studies was set up without the project coordinator getting his anticipated invitation.

3 Troubled waters: The project as agitation or distress

Mr Larchwood: What did Mr Pickford really mean when he said it all starts with you?

Pupil: Voting. We chose.

Mr Larchwood: Yes, that's what I think he meant. Anybody over 21 may vote. It may come down to 18.

Mr Pickford: There are some exceptions, Mr Larchwood.

Mr Larchwood: Exceptions?

Mr Pickford: Yes, Mr Larchwood. Have you any first-hand knowledge of them?

Mr Larchwood: Lunatics?

Mr Pickford: And felons actually undergoing a prison sentence.

Mr Larchwood: Mr Pickford has just given you the answer, I'm sure.

Mr. Pickford: Yes. Mr Larchwood, I've a real live lord living next to me.

Mr Larchwood: (interrupting) Just a quick point about the date of the general election. . . .

Mr Pickford: (mock indignation!) Do you want me to carry on, Mr Larchwood? Do you want me to take that point up?

Mr Larchwood: There is another danger, Frankie Howerd. Mr Pickford may already have pointed it out to you. Suppose George Best stood. Would he get elected?

Mr Pickford: And there is another danger. Influence. Bullying. So we have a voting system. Anybody know what it's called?

Pupil: Election?

Mr Larchwood: I think, Mr Pickford, you may get more response if you say 'voting by S.B.' By secret . . .?

Pupil: Secret box?

Mr Pickford: Very good.

What is functional in one context may be dysfunctional in another. In spite of the felt obligation to assent to a rhetoric of collaboration, the truth is that internal tensions within teams of teachers are unremarkable and normal. The competitive edge in the above example is readily visible. The analogy is with tag wrestling, or a tennis match in which the children are spectators while the teachers score off each other. Team teaching is an institutional apparatus that threatens privacy. It also exposes teachers to a second audience of potentially critical colleagues ('Yes, there is a certain amount of reserve; in fact I've had to sit through some of the lead lessons taken by my colleagues biting my upper lip and seething within; I must admit that at the petty level there is a certain amount of friction and niggling'). Many teachers expressed nervousness about the presence of other teachers ('I felt surprisingly shy').

There were, on the other hand, a number of 'selfish' reasons why trial school teachers felt that they had a vested interest in an increase in uncertainty. The Keele project actually made legitimate and gave institutional approval to certain kinds of uncertainty. The project opened up the possibility of novel or exotic career moves; it weakened bureaucratic control ('It's an outside run, you see; places me to some extent outside the hierarchy'); it allowed occupational self-identification as an innovator ('It is splendid to be in the van of educational progress'), and was an antidote to the general boredom and repetitiveness of life in schools.

Many trial school teachers sought new alliances, which seemed to offer new opportunities for bidding for scarce resources of prestige, time and money. Awareness of this joint bid was very acute, if general in scope ('The attitude of individual members of staff is so complex: some people seem to regard the existence of humanities as a kind of threat inside the school over resources; others see it as a threat to status, or graded posts, or something else; it's all so indefinite and vague that I can't pin it down'). The weakened bureaucratic control leads to *ad hoc* networks, pressure groups and individual 'moral entrepreneurs' seeking to re-establish control by ostracism, heavy-handed humour, and professional gossip. One school may serve as an example of ostracism and banter used as instruments of social control. It is a rural trial school which had evolved over time a sharp division between its two staff rooms. The 'upper' one is mixed, the 'lower' men only. The norms of the 'lower' staff room are those of the war veteran. At least one trial teacher thought he ought to serve a three-year apprenticeship in the 'upper' staff room before applying for membership of the 'lower' one. The general atmosphere of this NAS stronghold is rather like a trackside railwayman's hut. Banter and cynicism make legitimate genuine educational discussion, which is acceptable only when shorn of any element of idealism. In this lower staff room the Keele project had a rough ride ('They think it's nonsense and they tell us straight; the sportsmaster says integrated studies is a big skive'). But in the upper staff room 'among the knitters' the criticisms are more oblique ('It's really snide up top').

The issue of team 'leadership' is also a problem, linked as it is to the career structure of the profession and the possibility of 'departmental overlordships', as one feudally minded trial school teacher put it, in humanities. In one school a rhetoric of democracy masked real differences in principles or policies. In another a trial school teacher could not bring herself to use the name of her more dominant adversary, directing all her criticism at an abstract entity called 'the leader' ('The problem with the leader is that she has no time to listen'). In front of the integrated studies pupils they simulated unity and called each other by Christian names. The headmaster of the leader's school believes that leadership emerges naturally, like in the Tory party. Except his, of course.

But our guiding metaphor of troubled waters draws attention to the uncertainty, which is often valued for its own sake. The crowning glory of the Keele project was that it offered its imprimatur on the ensuing chaos, creating the taste by which it was enjoyed. Most appropriate garb for the curriculum visitor is a combat jacket and a floral tie.

4 The gift of grace: The project as salvation

In spite of the self-help rhetoric of grassroots curriculum development, many teachers welcomed the project as a kind of act of grace. Few teachers in fact had this response, but those that did had it in full measure (not only life, but life more abundant!). As a response it is curiously ambiguous. The teacher admits weakness, expresses belief, and is rewarded not only with assistance, but the certainty of belonging to the elect. The underlying metaphor is one more naturally embedded in non-conformist theology. Only sinners achieve salvation. Statements of profound inadequacy ('We're just groping in the dark') become closely associated with a feeling of being in the van of educational progress ('I like to feel in the front line in the fight for integrated studies'). Curiously this militant tone was rarely reflected in the project team. The Nuffield/Schools Council Humanities Curriculum Project under Laurence Stenhouse also detected a curious tendency for some of the trial school teachers to be more righteous than the scribes and pharisees at the centre. Of such is the kingdom of curriculum development.

But this imagery makes sharp demands upon the curriculum visitor. Not untypical is a 'confessional' tone, and a heightened set of demands on both sides, going way beyond the call of duty. Several teachers described cosy-sounding 'little chats' that they had with supportive coordinators. One saw the project as a twenty-four-hour crisis counselling service, not unlike the Samaritans. It was 'good' that the coordinator was 'on call every hour of the day and night, when needed'. One teacher described David Bolam as 'omnipresent'. Another claimed 'a resurrection of interest'.

The emphasis is on faith, and on the sustaining support of the faithful. Educational matters are best discussed out of school hours, if possible in circumstances recalling the Last Supper ('It ended up sort of meeting at weekends, in each others' houses and ringing each other up'). The biggest sin is to betray the innovation, seen too frequently as an affective commitment to crude central propositions ('It's those barriers between subjects, you see; we've got to break them down'). Appropriate garb for the curriculum visitor is a homespun tweed suit and a white shirt.

5 New props for identity: The project as theatre

'Well, yes, I use more swear words per week in the humanities lesson. The teachers and the kids feel rather outside the normal code of restraints. It even affects little points of style that one has . . . the way you move around the classroom, and that kind of thing.' (geography specialist, in trial school integrated studies team)

'If you've got a class, you're teaching. If you've got any other audience, you're performing. If you've got other members of staff, just as if parents came in on an open evening, well, that's a performance. Even if you are giving a demonstration of how you teach, its still a performance. Even though you're not conscious of it, influencing you, underneath it still would be. It's bound to be, because there are people there. And it's different. It's not a teaching situation. A teaching situation is staff–pupil.' (trial school teacher)

Within our fifth guiding metaphor the teacher is able to see the curriculum project quite simply as a theatre and a collection of props. He is an actor, and by manipulating the props can reconstruct his own professional identity. He may be seeking personal or political visibility or he may see contact with a Schools Council curriculum project as having career significance. Often this aspiration was quite explicit. ('When I move from here I hope my time with the Keele project will allow me to get a head of humanities in another school'). For the subject specialist who has abandoned the security of a subject for integrated studies, there may be a dilemma. He suspects that integrated studies is seen by headteachers as low-status knowledge, but believes that this is more than compensated by the value of the public label that reads 'curriculum innovator'. This lapel badge of the innovator is the most glittering bauble that a project can offer, which is why trial school teachers at a Keele project diffusion conference complained bitterly when an administrative oversight prevented the allocation of these baubles of identity, so that trial school teachers were indistinguishable from 'interested others'. But this merely shows how important such identification is. One teacher described how he had attended a diffusion conference. He carefully pointed out that it had been 'by invitation'. He found to his surprise and pleasure ('I found it very satisfying') that he was constantly pressed to talk of his trial school experiences to the 'ordinary-style teachers'. A particular pleasure was to come across Mr Carruthers, who knew him in less exotic days ('On meeting Mr Carruthers, he expressed astonishment at seeing me at any such conference, having remembered me perhaps as the most conventional teacher of his earlier life; he used to think me hidebound and said that I'd changed beyond all recognition; I admitted to being scarred [sic] by integrated studies. It's the biggest shake-up of my teaching I'm likely to experience').

But how are these stars and badges allocated? There are two

traditions, reflecting two different kinds of political aspiration. The first tradition is the war medal, the second tradition is the badge of the sheriff's deputy.

The war medal rewards past achievement. It is set firmly within the grassroots tradition. The project's task is to articulate and spread 'good practice' within schools. Its first task, therefore, is to select those schools where good practice is already rooted. Such schools 'help out'. The trial school teaches and the project learns. The teachers implicitly reject the top-down initiatives of the central team, preferring bottom-up signals. The project team may be busy bees, but the individual teachers, professional lords within their own classrooms, are the flowers. The war medal recognizes success. It is pinned on the school's collective chest, and its award is greeted with a round of applause on prize day. Even the most modest individual teacher may cling to this image, in spite of disclaiming noises ('Well if you really think that what we're doing here can help the project . . . then by all means; I feel one must always be willing to let others learn from one's experiences').

Not so the badge of the sheriff's deputy, which indicates future responsibility. The star suggests a delegated task ('We realized what a difficult assignment the Keele project was giving us'). The war veteran may swap the anecdotes of classrooms survival, but the sheriff's deputy saddles up his horse. He is culturally obliged to express routine modesty and doubt, but is expected to bring his man home in the end. The project becomes a 'challenge', a 'tremendous task', or even 'an excuse for trying out team teaching'. The man who forms the posse may himself just be going for the ride, but whose law and order does he serve? We have already suggested that some teachers became more dogmatic than the central team itself, although uncritically willing to label it 'expert'. Others used the star to undermine within-school curriculum policy, using the project as the 'different drummer'.

The project-as-theatre may generate several 'audiences': the project team, the local authority, and the local colleges. Some of these may be unwittingly cast in the role of the ideal spectator, arms spread wide in silent acknowledgment. Project visitors feeling that entrance into schools is best managed initially by handing out the war medals may actually represent the project team as spectators ('We're in your good hands'). The political repercussions work on two levels. The individual teacher has gained a toe-hold outside the conventional chain of command. But he has surrendered something of his autonomy and freedom of choice (at least during the trial period) to an agency not able to take account of local circumstances, or the particular group of pupils involved.

There is one area of inexplicable inactivity. As Shipman has already pointed out in Chapter 2, the typical trial school had little contact with other trial schools, except spasmodically over time, or in local pockets. One reason for this was that a number of headteachers denied the 'social usability strategy' view of curriculum development ('I wouldn't expect schools to influence each other; our main link is with Keele, but in the school I need to gain the attention of some of my own teachers'). Yet when these links occurred, they were widely praised ('I was amazed that Chapel Marten was doing that; had I known about it earlier I would have shown it to our kids, as a stimulus').

For the war veteran, the sheriff's deputy and the project central team, dress is within the options available to members of educational conferences (i.e. dark suits on the first day, jeans on the second, and pyjamas on the third). But the lapel badges must be large. A general purpose lapel badge is Richard Hamilton's 'Slip it to me', which can be worn by any party.

6 The free sample: The project as commercialism

The guiding metaphor here relates to models established within the commercial world. The curriculum visitor is seen as a 'representative', and the school's perception of the project is conditioned by the known or suspected link between the Schools Council and the commercial publishing houses. The status of the curriculum visitor is marginal, and his access to the staff room is grudging ('But where else can he lay out his wares?'). Even if a teacher retains 'specimen copies', there are no obligations associated with his consumer role, although the project-as-producer can easily run the gamut of consumer-protection entrepreneurs, who will, for example, pose as experts on levels of readability (one headteacher attained a level of expertise that enabled him to comment on levels of readability in terms of percentiles after a quick glance through a pack of materials).

But, however successfully our curriculum salesman operates, his role is a limited and limiting one. In particular the Keele project faced with such a viewpoint was not allowed to worry about whether its curriculum materials were being used in a way it would regard as appropriate. Misinterpretation becomes an inadmissible concept. There is only interpretation ('We are going to buy Keele material and Stenhouse material and make our own mix'). The project visitor is under some obligation to swap his briefcase for a suitcase, and go in for the hard sell. The word 'sell' frequently crops up in any conversation, often with derogatory overtones ('Most teachers have ideas of their own; all we need is someone to do the dog's work and provide the resources; fine, yes, isn't that what you are trying to sell?'). The curriculum salesman keeps his hair neatly trimmed and makes frequent visits to the cloakroom with a large ivory comb. And the Project Director looked forward to his post-project diffusion role with misgivings as there would be a hiatus between the end of the project and the publication of the packs ('I've got to sell the project next year and nothing in the bag, so to speak').

7 Ground bait: The project as exploitation

'I didn't know what I had let myself in for.' (trial school teacher)

Occasionally the free sample of goods and curriculum material may be perceived cynically as 'ground bait'. This view of the school-project link is distinguished by an increase in the expectation and practice of mutual distrust ('What people have suspected is that you have been sort of feathering your own nest; that's crude, I know, but the feeling is that you have been drawing on our experience and go on to produce something which you then present at Keele as your own; from time to time in comes a revision of the pack, and we find it's something that we thought of; we discussed it with you and then you put it in'). Both sides keep a dossier of evidence against the other, hoping to make what Garfinkel would call a 'successful denunciation' at the end of the exercise.

Some intrepid schools perceived the Keele project as bait all right, but elected to take the bait without the hook. This may be attempted in quite subtle ways. The curriculum visitor may be welcomed, as I was on one occasion, and characterized unhelpfully as a 'measurement man', but then asked to undertake a piece of testing or interviewing only marginally related to the Keele project ('Ah, Mr Jenkins, so glad you could come; we've got a little problem that you may be able to help with . . .'). Appropriate garb for such visits is a Uher 4000 Report L tape-recorder and supplementary gadgetry. Try to appear nonchalant, like a kitted-out fly-fisherman.

8 Management by objectives: The project as consultancy

'In the team here at school you find that there are two fairly distinct notions of what you are trying to do. One, you have a content-based notion in which the teacher is concerned largely that the children know certain facts. And the other is a notion of enquiry-based learning in which – certainly I think that's what the aim is. I tackled Mr Bolam once and got some sort of help. He seemed to say it was enquiry-based. But the coordinator seemed to think that Keele, in a sense, abdicated its responsibility for giving objectives in the pack itself. I've tried to get us all to pool ideas and pick out certain aspects similar to the development of a

theme exercise we did at the Keele meeting last weekend. But we
didn't really pick out key issues. We just sort of wandered,
serpent-like through a maze. A tapestry of issues. . . . I hope I'm
not being an intellectualist, but it doesn't seem to me that people
really care about educational issues. All they care about is whether
they can handle a class.' (trial school teacher)

Perhaps the most optimistic guiding metaphor is the management
consultancy one. A number of teachers saw contact with the Keele
project as an outside opinion, a way of helping schools to identify
and articulate underlying issues ('We welcome project visitors – it's
nice to have an outside opinion on the problems facing us'). Several
teachers felt that the project had usefully exposed some of their
unexamined assumptions ('It is difficult to define the ideas that we
actually hold; contact with the project was an eye-opener'). There
was some evidence, too, of the project being given a responsive role.
Project team members were welcomed because it gave trial school
teachers a chance to 'put Keele on the spot'. The coordinators were
praised for avoiding the dangers of 'armchair observation' ('There
was no armchair observation, but much discussion, much to-ing
and fro-ing'). Much of the strength of the guidelines to teachers
produced in the *Keele Integrated Studies Handbook* derived from the
willingness of trial school teachers to discuss issues. This is not to
say that everybody was satisfied. At least one teacher felt that Keele
had abdicated its responsibility. Having produced 'excellent content
and ideas' it neglected to face the more difficult pedagogical issues
(It's an area nobody seems clear about'). As late as June 1971 one
of the coordinators was taking a tough line at a team meeting on
this one ('We pay lip-service to the idea of pupils learning at their
own rate, but the project simply hasn't behaved in a way that
qualifies it to talk about individual pupils').

9 Cargo cult: The project as overwhelming technology

'We saw you as pack horses. Hey! That's a nice pun.' (trial school teacher)

Our final guiding metaphor is from social anthropology, suggested studies by the reaction of primitive communities to a contiguous highly technological culture. Cargo cults have in common a reaction to 'culture shock' expressed in bizarre beliefs about cargo. A plane or boat will arrive on the beach and distribute unlimited largesse. A number of trial school teachers developed irrational expectations and made wholly unreasonable demands on the Keele project. Curriculum materials, electronic gadgetry, dust-free chalk, stationery, individual study books, display material . . . there is no demand that the curriculum cargo cult fails to legitimate. Several schools informed the Keele project that it wished to receive curriculum material in areas identified by the school, the clear implication being that Keele would run its presses for this local need. At least one of the coordinators found herself seriously out of pocket in an effort to meet such expectations. 'No harm in asking, boy', said one of the offending departmental heads. Welsh, of course.

One anecdote may suggest the kind of flavour that became possible once the cargo cult movement gained momentum. A school booked a visit of a group of actors from the Derby Playhouse, who were to perform a social drama relevant to gypsies and other travellers, one of the fourth-year themes recommended by the Keele project. The players were booked at less than their usual professional rate on a calculation based on the school's ability to collect a reasonable sum per head. Meanwhile the coordinator offers to subsidize the school and also to invite a sister school free of charge – an arrangement that would involve very considerable personal expense. The head of the second school takes a harder line.

Why should he pay out of the school account? The show is free. Keele is meeting the bill.

The cargo cult metaphor places the school firmly within a culture of poverty, and the teachers' behaviour is based on a frank recognition of this fact. The easiest solution is to embrace the belief system that guarantees the goodies, but that doesn't help the school survive the disenchantment that follows the likely disconfirmation of its excessive expectations. But the cargo cult metaphor does not always lead to the writing of a *When Prophecy Fails* (Festinger, Riecken and Schachter 1956). For some the dream came true. Appropriate garb for the curriculum visitor is as for the driver of a fork-lift truck.

Implications for models of planned change

One or two tentative suggestions can be gleaned from the foregoing analysis. These should not be read in any sense as concrete recommendations, but as questions to be raised against the conventional wisdom of planned organizational change in education.

In the first place it must by now be clear that the usual RD & D (research development and dissemination) model would be an inaccurate reflection of how the Keele project actually operated. Not only was there no self-conscious division into stages, but the research element was almost entirely lacking. The project avoided approaching its central task comparatively. Schools were not invited to compare the benefits of an integrated studies approach against any named alternatives but to articulate the problems and possibilities of integrated studies as an 'alternative' approach involving new goals as well as new means. This shifted the thrust of school-based evaluation towards the internal logic of the programme and the kind of 'feel' it had in the classroom. Equally the project, like most first-generation curriculum projects, made little more than gestures in the direction of dissemination.

An alternative model, suggested by Hoyle (1972) and others,

gives four stages of innovation: *invention, development, diffusion* and *adoption*. This model works at two levels. In terms of the educational system at large it is not dissimilar to the RD & D model. In terms of the individual school, it is compatible with recent moves towards local or school-based curriculum development. Such school-based approaches depart from the conventional wisdom of trial followed by dissemination, and stress the self-sustaining process of curriculum renewal in the individual school. I suspect that underlying Shipman's account is a willingness to consider the Keele project as the first example of a cellular rather than a centre-peripheral curriculum project. His account suggests, crudely, that the attempt failed, at least in so far as the publishing tasks pulled the coordinators towards the centre. Although the changes in organization within the project suggest that this drift occurred, a closer look at the processes of invention, development, diffusion and adoption hint otherwise. The fine tracery of the argument that could be developed does not add up to a rebuttal of Shipman's central thesis. But at least we are left with an ambiguity:

Invention   The Keele project was never a package. Teachers perceived it as a loose umbrella for their own inventiveness, often in a way that the project found embarrassing. In the absence of an understood overarching theory, reinterpretation was also possible on the conceptual level.

Development The project produced exemplary units, based on the view that integrated teaching within the humanities is viable within a number of alternative forms. The innovation (in spite of the emphasis on large themes and team teaching) proved in practice to be surprisingly divisible. Schools selected amended and extended at will.

Diffusion   More significant than end-of-project diffusion was local growth, frequently within a particular school. The first target audience was frequently the trial

Adoption

school teachers' immediate colleagues. This in spite of the fact that between-school contact within the Keele project was sporadic. People learn more from their own experience than the experiences of others. The problem of adoption and institutionalization was a long-term one fought largely within the individual school. The Keele project, like a wooden horse of Troy, was left within the gates. The implicit climates of approval and disapproval were already there inside the school. We have seen how many teachers, faced with the problems of adopting, chose to adapt, thus avoiding the ecological trap (the existing rules for coping with the complexities of the environment). In doing so they called into question their own frameworks of social comparison. In the phenomenology of curriculum development, would-be fathers still apply to the socially validated adoption societies. But they come away with their own children.

It seems clear that future attempts to monitor the reinterpretation of curriculum projects will need more sophisticated models of the school-project interaction than are currently available. These impressions are a stumbling attempt to identify some of the problems that will have to be faced. It may well be that the reference orientations that are established by the various participants, and the perceptions by which such issues as marginality are determined, crucially affect the progress and implementation of educational innovation.

7. Impact and survival

The research on which this book is based was not concerned with the evaluation of the curriculum materials produced or with the merits of integrated studies. It was concerned with those factors in schools that affect the impact of a project, both during the trial years, and immediately afterwards. There is therefore no measure of the success or failure of the Integrated Studies Project as an exercise in curriculum development. The period covered was of a trial. Schools were under no obligation to continue with the innovation once that trial period had finished. Furthermore, in this project, where there was no blueprint for schools to follow, it was very difficult to establish any satisfactory criteria of success or failure. The conventional evaluation was organized partly by the project team and partly through an observers' panel of local authority advisers and college of education lecturers, not part of the project team and using their own judgement of what they saw in the schools visited.

Behind the hunches that are investigated in this chapter lies a simple economic idea. Change in any organization requires some investment, whether of ideas, of resources, of time or of energy. The chances of that change becoming established and having a lasting impact probably depends on the level of investment made. In schools this investment would consist of organizational changes primarily instigated by the headteacher, and of investments of time and energy by the teachers involved in the trial. In addition there would be resources pumped into the school by the project team and by the local authorities concerned.

Investment and impact

The first part of this chapter is concerned with impact in this purely economic way. It is an attempt to relate what was put into the project by those involved to the changes in the schools by the end of the trial period. But these changes were not measured only by references to changes in curriculum in an integrated direction. Early taped discussions with groups of teachers indicated that there would be divergent consequences. Efforts were made to measure spin-off effects from the introduction of the new ideas across the period of trial. Once again, there is no concern with the content or quality of the work done in these trial schools. The major part of this chapter is concerned with the hunch that the impact of a curriculum development project is closely related to the effort that is put in at the start and during its early implementation.

The second hunch that is investigated is again drawn from an economic model. It is assumed that planned curriculum change is similar to the giving of aid to developing countries. In each case investment is made in the hope that there will be a breakaway from traditional methods and finally a movement into self-sustained growth, making investment from the outside unnecessary. This view derives from the work of Rostow (1966) who has traced the way traditional societies break into self-sustained economic growth through the build-up of investment to a point where there are sufficient resources to generate further investment from inside. [1]

It is assumed that schools, like countries with subsistence economies, often exhaust all available resources in just keeping going. Survival is itself a triumph. The breakthrough into self-sustained growth will depend on a combination of motivation to innovate by at least a minority and their ability to mobilize sufficient resources to introduce and sustain new methods, often in the face of opposition from groups supporting old procedures. Teaching leaves little energy over for thought and action to change procedures. In many schools changes in routine bring problems of discipline and performance. As in traditional societies everyday routines are defended because they are the means of survival and have become part of the identity of those involved. Curriculum projects are seen in this chapter as the equivalent of aid programmes to promote economic growth. There may be a disturbing parallel between the failure of such aid programmes to effect pump-priming in developing countries and the short-lived impact of curriculum innovations once the supporting projects have been disbanded.

To obtain a valid measure of the impact of investment by schools and teachers on organization and curriculum, it was necessary to define and measure indices of investment at the start of the project. Once it was known which schools were successful in sustaining innovation, there would be a danger that this would be taken as indicating a high level of investment. The measures of investment were made therefore in a crude form in 1969 and 1970. They were then amended in 1971, where necessary. When the impact of the project was measured at the end of 1971, these investment indices could be used without too much contamination through knowledge of the way in which the schools had changed.

The lasting impact on the curriculum and organization of the schools was assessed in the term following the trial period. Ideally this length of time should have been greater, but the longer the intervening period between the end of trial and the measure of impact, the more difficult was it to detect whether the project experience had been responsible for a change or whether the many other changing factors affecting the school had been more responsible. Full details of the research procedures and the measures used can be found in the Appendix.

The impact of the project

The first measure of the performance of a school during the trial was defined merely as the fulfilment of the initial obligation, the contract, to try out integrated studies across the trial period. The three indices of the time and energy invested by teachers were based on attendance at meetings, accumulation of supplementary materials and the provision of feedback to the project. These were combined with the investment by the school, as indicated by the provision of a special team leader, adjustments to the timetable and the provision of special planning time for the integrated studies team, to see whether there was a relation between the effort put in and the fulfilment of the contract to trial.[2] As each of these six indices were measured on three-point scales, the maximum score for any school was eighteen and the lowest six. The table that follows shows the total scores on this combined index for the thirty-eight schools that were involved.

	Investment Score
22 schools completing 2 years of trial as contracted	14·0
4 schools leaving to continue their own version of integrated studies	14·0
7 schools dropping out before completing contracted trial	6·9
5 schools joining the project in the second trial year	15·4

This table merely indicates that the chance of a school successfully fulfilling its contract was largely determined by the outlay of time, effort and resources made by the teachers involved. This is obvious, but the need to invest, plan and manage by the schools before the introduction of new curriculum is often neglected. However great the investment by the sponsoring agent and the project team, long-term success of innovation depends on efforts made in the schools. The key to effective innovation may lie in mobilizing teachers and providing the conditions in which their enthusiasm can be fired and manifested in the investment of personal time and effort. The high investment by schools joining the trial in the second year, 1970–1, probably indicates that the project team realized the need to obtain this high level of investment as a result of experiences in the first trial year.

The impact on the curriculum was measured along four three-point scales described in the Appendix. These measured the amount of trial material in use after the end of the trial period, developments arising from the trial in integrated studies, developments in the related fields of the humanities, and the persistence of some form of team teaching. The breadth of these measures is accounted for by early observations that schools tend to focus their attention and energies on particular and often peripheral aspects of the innovation, rather than implementing it in the way anticipated by the project team. By the end of the trial period aspects that had appeared secondary to the project team had become of primary concern to the teachers in the schools. The indices were attempts to measure some of this spin-off effect. The table shows the relation between the curriculum impact and the various investments and contexts provided within the school. x indicates little or no relation. The significance levels indicate the probable existence of a relation. The smaller the figure the more is a relation probable.

Outputs	Inputs					
	2a	2b	2c	2d	3a	3b
Contractual success	0·01–0·001	0·01–0·001	x	x	x	0·01–0·001
Curriculum success	0·05–0·02	0·01–0·001	x	x	x	x

The significance of the effort put in by the teachers (2a) and of the special arrangements made by the school (2b) all point to the importance of investment in innovation. The measure of organizational climate (3b), derived from Halpin (1966), was also centred on the enthusiasm of the teachers, and this was in turn related to the amount of effort they were putting in. The most predictive indices for persistence of curriculum change within the measures used were the feedback of information to the project, the accumulation of supplementary materials by teachers and the provision of planning time by the school. It is misleading to suggest that these indices were separable into teacher and school investments. In the case of time for team planning meetings particularly, provision by the school had to be accompanied by effort by the teachers. The conditions for innovation could be provided but could only be used to good effect through the efforts of the teachers.

The attempt to compress the variety of responses to a curriculum project within a table of figures is grossly misleading. This applies particularly to the Keele Integrated Studies Project, where the intention was for schools to develop in their own way under the broad framework provided by the team. There was no clear definition of what could constitute success or failure. It was possible to predict the impact of a project from the effort put in, but the nature of that impact was unpredictable. In this kind of project, and probably in all projects, the accidental spin-off effects may be more important than the central objectives pressed by the project team. It may be the catalytic effects of projects that are important, rather than the more limited impact of their specific curriculum objectives. This is a hopeful view, if frustrating to curriculum planners. Apparent failures to innovate as judged by a quick reference to the implementation of project objectives may actually be successes in other aspects visible only after closer inspection. Project rejection is probably less of a problem than project transmutation, and the latter may not be a problem.

Schools gave different emphasis to the principles of integration and the methods through which integrated work could be organized. Many more were concerned merely with bridging subjects or with using common themes, or with introducing some form of humanities teaching, than with using subjects as tools as recommended by the project team. This was the result of the reluctance of schools to consider the underlying principles behind integration. They were far more concerned with the practical implementation of some form of integrated studies in their schools.

The consequent variety was staggering. One school had done an elaborate paste and scissors job to produce a collection of materials combined from both Keele and humanities projects, violating the principles of both but providing an effective resource. Other schools concentrated their efforts on organizing team teaching. Others focused on enquiry-based work and the preparation of materials for it. Others decided that the crucial reorganization must be in the organization of resources. The innovation was centred on a room full of cornflake boxes in one school. Even in those schools where the direct impact of the project had been minimal it was possible to trace effects, usually on the timetable or on plans for the raising of the leaving age. These could be as slight as the idea of team meetings to coordinate the work of teachers pursuing their own subject interests. This often spread to groups of teachers not involved in the trial. At the other extreme it could involve a complete reorganization of the timetabling in the school to ensure the maximum of project-based work. None of these were directly traceable to the project, but the teachers and headteachers in interviews stressed that the experience of trial had been an important factor in preparing for the reorganization.

The limelight schools

The second hypothesis examined was that there was a threshold of investment beyond which a school would break through into self-sustained innovation. In the first months of the project, after the first collection of indices of investment, it was predicted that nine schools were in this category. Perhaps the best way of examining the impact of full participation in a curriculum project is through examining this hypothesis and the impact on these nine schools.

In one school, which had apparently invested heavily in the first term of the trial, the impact measured after the end of the trial two years later was negligible. The reason given in interviews with the teachers involved was that the school was engaged in the reorganization of the local school organization, and this had to take priority. This reason was given in all the schools in this area that were involved in this reorganization. Schools quite justifiably concentrate their energies on the most immediate task. What was disappointing in this particular case was that the two years of trial appeared to have had no direct impact at all. There were no concrete plans to pick the work up again and no signs that team teaching, enquiry-based methods, the systematic projection and storage of resources would be revived once the reorganization had been completed. Secondary reorganization appeared to have erased the concrete experience of being involved in the project. There was a tribute to the ideas presented and a hope that later on the work would be picked up again, but meanwhile there were more basic things to do, particularly ensuring that standards of work did not fall.

In one other school, which had initially invested so much that self-sustained innovation was predicted, there was only a slight impact. Here the rapid fall-off of interest at the end of the trial had been manifested in a rapid reduction from seven to two in the number of teachers involved in integrated work. Incongruously, the reason seemed to be the enthusiasm of the team leader. While the trial was in progress, this enthusiasm had held the team together, but once the trial finished most of the teachers decided to go back to straight subject teaching. The problem here was probably in the methods used to assess investment. In practice much of this effort had not been made by all the teachers involved, but mainly by the team leader. In the remaining seven schools the initial heavy investment did seem to have led to greater confidence in the teachers as they reorganized for the raising of the school leaving age, and as they prepared for secondary reorganization. In two, however, this confidence appeared only in the teachers who had been involved in the project, which remained isolated within the school. In the other five, the experience gained on the project seemed to have had the effect of reinforcing the efforts of the teachers involved so that they could now plan their future work with confidence and without outside help. The experience of trial was obviously not exclusively responsible for this, but seemed to have reinforced it.

It would be wrong to suggest that even in five out of thirty-eight schools the experience of trial had created a breakthrough. But there had been an increase in confidence in handling curriculum innovation. This did not necessarily mean that these schools would now change rapidly. Indeed, these teachers were now able confidently to resist innovation. But all were actively reviewing their curriculum and had not only thought out where they were going but how they would get there. This only involved radical reorganization in one school. In the rest, innovations initially organized from outside had been incorporated into a policy thought out by the staff. The experience with integrated studies had been an important factor in building up this ability to assess and plan.

High-level manpower (2c)

It was predicted that the participation of heads, deputies and heads of departments in teams responsible for starting integrated studies would increase the chance of the school fulfilling its contract on the trial and of maximum impact on the curriculum. However, the actual result of the involvement of high-level manpower was to reduce the chances of influences from the trial surviving. There seemed to be two conflicting influences at work. When the heads of departments were considered their involvement seemed to be beneficial. The involvement of deputy heads seemed to have no effect. But the influence of the headteacher's participation seemed to be negative.

This tendency for the participation of heads to reduce the impact of the innovation seemed to result partly from its association with the press-ganging described earlier. Three of the seven schools that failed to complete the trial were in this category and had heads who had initially joined the integrated studies team. However, this was only a partial explanation. Even where there had been prior consultation with a willing or enthusiastic staff, the involvement of the head seemed to inhibit genuine innovation. The teachers interviewed suggested that it was difficult to take the initiative when the head was participating as a team member. Secondly they explained that the head often had to withdraw from team teaching because other business had unexpectedly cropped up. The most successful teams were usually centred around two or three enthusiastic volunteers. The presence of a head seemed to dampen this enthusiasm.

The material environment (2*d*)

The apparent irrelevance of the physical conditions of the schools involved was also unexpected. This may have been the result of using blunt instruments to measure facilities. The observers' panel reporting at the end of the project found that inadequate resources were important in determining the discontinuation of integrated studies, particularly in small schools. But apparently squalid and badly equipped schools seemed to have coped as well as lavishly endowed glass palaces. Yet this was a project that called for material resources, audio-visual supports and rooms suitable for groups of various sizes involved with team teaching. It was not pleasant having to use a hall still smelling of school lunch, but older schools often had odd spaces and huts and were less worried about the noise and the movement that goes with enquiry-based work. Above all, the absence of physical resources was unimportant compared with the enthusiasm of staff.

Previous experience of integrated studies (3a)

Experience of some sort of integrated studies teaching before joining the project appeared to make little difference to the final impact
of the trial. Of nineteen schools with developed courses before trial
in the humanities field, four dropped out early. In these cases the
trial seems to have stopped further innovation. Of ten schools
entering the trial without any previous experience in this field, two
dropped out early. However, all four schools that left the project
early to carry on with their own version had previous experience
in the integrated direction. These schools preferred their own,
already localized work. The initiative of those twenty-two schools
who stayed with the trial throughout the two years of trial was also
in this local direction after the finish.

These results are difficult to interpret. Previous experience was
hard to detect. Many schools were merely flirting with the integration of history and geography with junior forms or with humanities teaching for school leavers. The four schools in which the
experience of trial, however brief, seemed to have finished off even
the existing innovation were probably reluctant or uncertain in
their efforts to change their curriculum. The extra effort required
in the trial was enough to force a decision. However, these were
the schools where heads had shown greater enthusiasm than teachers
or where their selection had resulted from the hope of local advisers
that the trial would reinforce the first tentative steps towards innovation. A curriculum project works on the assumption that trial
schools will work towards objectives established as part of the trial.
But the schools and those responsible for them have other objectives
and the motives for joining are too varied for statistics to mean much.

The unpredicted factors

After the end of the trial period in the autumn of 1971, several
factors not initially predicted to be important were found to be

influential in determining the success of the project. The extent of press-ganging by enthusiastic heads has already been described. This was associated with, although not completely responsible for variations in the level of commitment to the trial. Schools ranged from those undertaking major reorganization to those who did not realize they were in a trial situation or insisted that they were just helping out.

Staff turnover

Two of the seven schools that failed to fulfil their contract of trial and five of the twenty-two that did complete lost over half their integrated studies teams across the two years in the project. In three of the five schools where high investment by the school had resulted in little change in the curriculum at least half of each team had left. In one school all seven of the team that joined in 1969 had left by 1972. Loss of staff on this scale finished the innovation.

However, staff turnover was not all loss. Seven teachers had left trial schools between 1969 and 1972 to start or take over the organization of integrated studies in other schools. Behind this spread lay the current interest in integration across the curriculum. Projects are set up to develop new approaches in areas of the curriculum where there is some agreement that change is desirable or where a trend has already started. The final impact depends on the strength of this tide as well as the effectiveness of the project itself.

Size of team

No predictions of the optimum size of team could be predicted from early meetings with teachers in the trial schools. Neither did the actual sizes of teams seem to be related to the impact of the project. The interpretation of team and team teaching varied widely. There was at one extreme a team of fourteen teachers loosely cooperating with a core at the centre of three keen heads of departments. At the other extreme was a one-man team who had taken on a number of subject areas himself. There was, however, some agreement among the teachers and heads who were involved that once the team got bigger than half a dozen, the number of organizational difficulties increased fast and the initial enthusiasm of volunteers was dissipated.

External and internal crises

In two schools that dropped out before finishing the trial there were major crises that had nothing particularly to do with the project. As teachers got involved in the crises within their school, they gave up integrated studies with the full agreement of the project team. These were both exceptional cases. There were also difficulties in two of the five local authority areas engaged in secondary reorganization. To innovate alongside such organizational changes was difficult. This applied particularly where the age of entry into the school was being changed. In one area with six trial schools, the introduction of middle schooling and entry to secondary schooling at 12 years effectively put an end to integrated studies in junior forms. The secondary schools were playing safe and concentrating on traditional subjects as an insurance against their fear of a less well-prepared intake.

In one school the appointment of a head of integrated studies had actually caused the dropping of the project. The reason for this was that a team that had cooperated from the start was disturbed by the appointment of a head of department who had very different ideas on how integrated studies should be organized. In this case a high investment by the school had resulted in the collapse of the innovation. There was another similar case. Here, an enthusiastic headteacher had formed a team in which he was to play an important part. But later this did not prove possible and the team of teachers rapidly shifted the basis of innovation from that

F

suggested by Keele to another supported by one vigorous and innovatory teacher within that team.

The statistical presentation of results conceals the real changes in the teachers who had been involved, and through them in the children. These changes ranged from a rejection of any form of integrated studies to enthusiastic acceptance. Here are four teachers summing up their experience in the trial:

> My teaching is now more relaxed, more flexible. This is naturally passed on to benefit pupils. I have a greater respect for more creative studies and the contribution that other teachers can make. It set the team thinking what to teach and to devise a course to that end. We will never again just accept a syllabus and separate subjects.

> The work imposed greater demands on teachers' time than normal classroom teaching. In the end we decided that it was harming other work and we gave it up. I enjoyed taking part in this project and am sorry it is over. But the pupils were losing out.

> I now know and acknowledge that my business is children, not English.

> I'm pleased I joined but I'm just as pleased that I've been demobbed.

◆◆ Comments by D. R. Jenkins

[1] Personally I don't find this analogy attractive. It appears to be based on the view that investment generates a capacity for further investment. The mechanism that makes this an economic truth depends in part on rates of interest. I can identify no parallel truth in curriculum innovation. A better analogy may be with side bets. The greater the commitment of resources the greater the motivation to succeed. A school goes out on a limb. It backs its judgement.

It refuses to hedge its bets. These are circumstances in which it has few convincing exit lines.

[2] The 'contract' is of course metaphorical, and its conditions, however reasonable, come out of Shipman's definition. In practice schools were accepted on different conditions, although the differences were rarely explicit. The style of negotiation resembled horse-trading. An earlier chapter noted how there was even some uncertainty in schools about whether they were trial schools or not. The argument wasn't about obligations, but about labels.

D. Bolam

8. The experience of the project

My immediate reaction is that Shipman has said it all and said it well. What to us was a press of problems, he has set out as a coherent story. In doing so, he has clarified their significance not only in a way that I find convincing, but in a way that will offer guidelines to future workers, which we lacked. And yet there are aspects of the project that he was not in a position to observe, and some that he saw from a different vantage point.

The shock to the system

Close as were Shipman's contacts with the project, he was not a member of the team and not actually involved in the work. His account needs to be counterpointed with what it felt like from the inside. I say 'felt' deliberately, as one cannot stress too strongly the emotional impact of the job, especially in the early stages. All of us experienced it as a 'shock to the system'.

At least part of the shock was that it was so different from the job we had been engaged on up till then. All of us had been teachers. Now we were trying to influence the situation, but from the outside: through teachers, by suggestions, and without direct or continuous contact with pupils. And even if we had decided to undertake more direct trials of methods and materials than we did, we would still only have been temporary guests in somebody else's classroom.

A number of people, of course, attempt to influence classrooms from the outside. Headmasters do, and LEA advisers, but as a project we had none of their power. Again, HMIs may wish to encourage change, though without 'direct power' to effect it, but we had none of their status. Besides, all these people are members of the establishment. It was our problem that we were not just attempting to make change from outside, but that we were seen as outside the system.

Or at least we were new members of it. Some turned to us with hope, but probed less about integrated studies than about what support they could, or could not, expect from us. Others (and sometimes the same people) were apprehensive, and wanted to find out the limits of our interference. Thus the important meetings between project members, LEA advisers, heads of potential trial schools, and key members of staff, had an important novelty about them. Previously discussions of change had involved only three of these four components, and perhaps involved only two of them at any point of time. The new situation was essentially more public, and the three regulars – advisers, heads, teachers – wanted to find out what the newcomers added up to, quite apart from what wares they were selling. They might indeed prefer to home-produce those wares themselves if the new situation seemed to offer more restriction than support. It cannot be over-stressed that the process of change was innovatory – and hence, disturbing and needing watching – every bit as much as the intended change area itself.

In one sense, however, the proclaimed policy of the Schools Council was not to initiate changes but only to encourage and develop changes that were already taking place. And Shipman rightly notes that some of the early project statements carry this coloration. Like anybody else, we claimed to be 'furthering growth points'. To say this of integrated studies was naïve, if not dishonest. What we finally came to see as our approach went far beyond supporting developments already there and made extreme demands on the school. The full force of the impact was continually softened anyway by our insistence on flexibility – on encouraging each school to work out its own salvation. This is not the place to elaborate – and Shipman has touched on several of the points already – but a list may suggest the 'shock' of what we were attempting:

1 The established growth points for 'integrated studies' were in primary schools or in courses for early leavers. The brunt of the project's work came to be in the first two forms of secondary schools and across the ability range.

2 The project's view of integrated studies – with its stress on subjects as distinctive tools of enquiry, deployed in the exploration of a large and complex theme – was in contrast to the popular one, where talk of 'breaking down subject barriers' sometimes concealed indifference to subjects.

3 A reformer of an established school subject is attempting to modify what is already there—textbooks, syllabuses, timetable time, public examinations, specifically trained teachers, etc. Integrated studies – as it is not an accepted part of the educational system – needs to establish its position and develop such support. Consequently, its introduction needs an above average amount of investment.

4 Reform in an individual school subject can go forward with minimal repercussions on the rest of the school (or at least we like to believe so). Integrated studies affects several subjects by definition, raises questions about the timetable, room use, staffing, and the deployment of resources, to say nothing of evaluating pupil achievement. In addition, changes in the 'humanities' not only stir sensitivities about values and public opinion, but press towards a reassessment of a large area of the curriculum.

5 A number of the recommendations – team teaching, group work, enquiry work in the neighbourhood – modify interpersonal relations within the school and the relation of the school to its local community in ways that went far beyond the domain of integrated studies. It seems the one certain thing of

curriculum developers that they will launch far more changes –
for good or for ill – than they ever intended to.

A project on integrated studies, then, presented schools with a
double novelty: in the procedure of change and in the area of
change. Schools could, of course – as suggested above – cushion
the shock by accepting our insistence on flexibility. This might
mean limiting their commitment to integrated studies, or by inter-
preting it – as Shipman shows in some of his most disturbing sections – in a way that made sense to them at the price of making little
sense of the project. But this is to overlook the extent that schools
were disturbed all the same. It also overlooks the fact that the real
cushions of shock were the team members. This is said in no sense
of self-pity (and personally I never faced this in the head-on way
that the coordinators did), but rather to use what it felt like on the
inside as evidence of a process.

At first sight, the phenomenon is the familiar one of being scape-
goats. This is to over-simplify and to put stress on the abrasive
aspects (and I am not sure that it wasn't the Schools Council that
became our mutual whipping boy! Of course, all team members
had to listen to many harsh comments. These were generally aimed
against the 'impracticability' of our plans and the density of our
language, rather than against integrated studies. But it was a situation where one's friends could impose as much strain as one's foes.
Certainly, in the early days there was a good deal of over-expecta-
tion (and there is still the feeling abroad that a Schools Council
project will come up with all the answers) and, even worse – as
Shipman makes abundantly clear – of conflicting expectations. Add
the point (also stressed by Shipman) that the coordinators were
treated as the standard-bearers of both the Schools Council and the
University of Keele without feeling themselves closely linked with
either, and one begins to get a sense of the personal stress on individuals. The experience pressed against our individual limitations
to a degree that we would not even admit to each other.

At least, this was all true at the start. One can take a good deal of strain if one has the security of a supporting professional situation and if one knows what one is trying to do. But in the early weeks and months, we had not settled down as a working team, and had only a slowly emerging idea of where we were going. And it is to this period that the discussion turns.

The long run-in: (a) working relations

The early months of the project are unavoidably the most confused and, hence, the most difficult to write about. They are also the one period of the project that Shipman cannot write about from inside observation. His close contact dates, as he says, from September 1967 – twenty-one months after the project began. He informed himself as thoroughly as he could from our papers and conversations, but this is the one period where one may be commenting on discussions he was not sitting in on.

One of the most obvious and urgent needs was for us to settle down as a team. The staggered nature of appointments and release meant that the full team was not assembled before September 1968 – i.e. after eight months. Long before this, however, difficulties had begun to emerge from two sources. First, the wish to be an efficiently working team was delayed by a bald fact – we were untrained people for undefined jobs – 'crass amateurs', as one team member put it at our last meeting. The novelty of the process as well as the novelty of the curriculum area both underline this, and the rapidity of transition made things worse. In one month we were confidently teaching a subject, in the next educationalists were expecting us to be experts in the nature of knowledge and teachers assumed we knew all about school organization. This is one of the things we insisted on in a final report to the Schools Council:

> On the issue of job definition, a pilot project could have been extremely helpful in providing a sharper description of what the future work would consist of, and of desirable specialization

within the team. As it was, the people concerned with appointments could only look out for such general considerations as personal acceptability to other teachers, and evidence of successful classroom teaching. Certainly much more needs to be done in analysing what are some of the skills required in work of this kind, and one cannot go on assuming that they are vaguely those of a good teacher.

As for training, we feel that this is a central responsibility of the Schools Council, and that it must consider ways and means of training members of projects in basic research techniques (e.g. the drawing up of a questionnaire or an observation schedule) as well as an understanding of curriculum theory. The increasing number of teachers studying for advanced diplomas, and other higher educational qualifications, will help but not entirely answer the need. It may be that the first term of a project's life should be seen solely as a training and definition exercise.

Slowly, of course, we worked out our own salvation. Some idea of how tasks were allocated within the team can be gained from the following pages. A second complication, however, deserves comment: the tension between the political origins of the team and the needs of integrated studies. The strategic advantages of having a coordinator in each LEA area, supported by the authority and (in all but one case) seconded from the local school have rightly been stressed by Shipman, and one could well see this as a useful model for curriculum development in other parts of the country. When it came to appointments, however, each LEA naturally wished to assure itself first and foremost that the coordinator for its area was a lively but tactful person, good in personal relationships and unlikely to antagonize heads or teachers. Yet it was also important for the project that members had, between them, experience across a range of schools and of subject areas. In the event, we satisfied the former but ended up with two teachers of English, two of history, and none of geography.

Such a difficulty could be overcome by the valuable assistance

we had from specialist teachers at a later stage, but another aspect
of the arrangement proved more immediately threatening. The
problem arose from the simple fact that two of us were based at
Keele, and the four coordinators were away and separated from
each other. This strained both individuals and the team. During the
early months, when coordinators were concentrating almost entirely on investigating work in their area, they found themselves
painfully isolated. To meet this problem, we found it necessary to
have a regular weekly team meeting at Keele, which ran on for
almost the full day. The need of contact with each other was
paramount, and we also needed to work over together the ideas
that were emerging. A more acrimonious reason for this set meeting
was an understandable fear by the coordinators that key decisions
would be made by the pair of us at Keele, and they would simply
be the 'office boys'. Sadly, I don't think we ever wholly overcame
this division within the team. And the two of us at Keele certainly
had advantages. Not only were we both closely linked with the life
of the university in a way the coordinators were too scattered to be,
but also we were free to be nationally mobile, and we had the more
direct knowledge of what other Schools Council projects were
doing as well as more contacts with the central personnel.

   This leads on to a second and complementary problem. Just as
individuals need the support of the membership of a team, so do
projects need to feel part of the larger organization – in this case
the Schools Council. Ideally, the central body needs to offer a team
at least three things: its interest and encouragement; practical advice
and expertise drawn from the range of projects it is supporting; and
a significant curriculum framework, i.e. an awareness of the contribution of a project's work to the total situation and its relationship to cognate projects. Shipman has commented on the slow
forming of links between the project and the council. Really, however, the problem was wider (and presumably was experienced by
most projects). The Schools Council was itself in a difficult position.
It had its own teething troubles. Like the rest of us, it was learning
as it went along and had little experience to draw on, beyond that

of Nuffield (who jointly funded some projects), and of the United States (to which at least one joint-secretary was despatched on a fact-finding mission!). Moreover, caution had to be the watchword to avoid any suggestion of a central body 'imposing' (to use a word used more than once by members of the advisory committee) a curriculum. The days of a status committee to explore the curriculum were far off. So what happened? Looking back, an extraordinary amount of time seems to have been spent linking up with other projects. Over the pints of beer, the three needs got some sort of satisfaction: there is a general sense of solidarity, a probing for working tips, and a questioning of demarcations.

In this context, a later event – outside the project – can be seen as important: the Scarborough Conference of June 1969, held eighteen months after we had started. This conference, called by the Schools Council, brought together representatives of all the main development projects. It improved morale, disseminated experience, and showed at least the council's concern for a fuller look at the whole curriculum. Inconclusive as so much of the discussion was, one can see why it was felt important enough to be published as Working Paper No. 33 (Schools Council 1971).

The Scarborough Conference was important in another way. It also included a number of heads especially concerned with innovation, and a representative from at least one examining board. Concerns about the life of the team and its links with the Schools Council – pressing as they seemed – are of less importance than the project's relation with all the other educational institutions who are involved in bringing about change. Shipman's clarification of this aspect seems to me to be extremely valuable. It is a good example of an observer seeing more of the game, especially as he followed up his contacts with the team by his questioning of advisers, heads and teachers. All could be left as said, were it not that one of his points surprises me: namely, the function of a teachers' centre at Keele. Shipman sees this as central to our original strategy and argues that it failed because neither the Schools Council nor the LEAs would grant funds for it. As I remember, it was an idea not of the project, but of the Director of the Keele Institute – and significantly the first approach for funds was before the team ever met. Understandably, the Director was looking at the total situation and the long term. He felt that a teachers' centre (on the analogy of the then recently founded one for modern languages) would nourish in-service work in the area and help humanities developments after the project finished. As for money, if we had really seen the centre as vital, we could have deployed sufficient project funds to sustain it. I even question whether such an idea would have meant decentralization, but rather that everything would have taken place at Keele. The genuine decentralization, which emerged during the project, and which we should have encouraged far more, was the meetings of teachers from several trial schools in a local teachers' centre or at a trial school, when progress was analysed. Shipman's point, of course, was not geographic – whether things happened at Keele or in the localities – but to make a distinction between two possible ways forward:

(a) Teachers fully cooperating in the development from the start, including the defining of aims.
(b) Teachers only helping a project to try out its materials and its suggested methods.

We had hoped for the first, but Shipman is doubtless right in suggesting that what happened was closer to the second – with teachers sometimes significantly modifying our ideas. To see the thing in perspective would require a side glance at another locally based project (North West Development Project), which was more successful in teacher release and the use of teachers' centres for development work; but it would also call for the scrutiny of why teachers' centre wardens in many parts of the country still find it very difficult to launch development groups, for all that teachers may be very concerned about change within their own schools.

The long run-in: (b) deciding on a strategy

What lies behind all these things – the team's life, relations with the Schools Council, cooperation with teachers and other people concerned – was the determination of the project's strategy. Strategy, in this sense, must include its understanding of integrated studies, its definition of appropriate teaching approaches, the delimitation of its task in terms of age groups and ability range, decisions about materials and themes to develop, to say nothing about the setting of a realistic timetable for its own efforts. This was not a clear-cut, one-off operation, but an untidy affair, involving bargaining as much as abstract definition, a victim of more than one uneasy modification. One may get some idea of what was involved by spotlighting two occasions (and statements) from the period June–July 1968, i.e. six months after the project started, but two months before the full team came together.

(1) MEMORANDUM FROM THE SCHOOLS COUNCIL TO THE PROJECT DIRECTOR (JUNE 1968)
Circumstances
The Schools Council had been late in making links with the team, and when it did, it felt we were attempting too much and were out of touch with teachers. When challenged, one of the joint secretaries offered the following definition of strategy.

Document: Possible guidelines for the Keele project

Stage I
Definition of integration and statement of its advantages as an approach to the humanities different from the single subject approach.

Stage II
Evidence from schools. What do they mean by integration? Examples of good practice, examination of objectives, achievements and difficulties. Working with groups of teachers,

attempt some kind of consensus as to areas where teachers would like a supporting service and appropriate age ranges.

Stage III

Take one or two of these areas perhaps corresponding to different age ranges and different degrees of integration and:

(*a*) Devise a fairly detailed scheme including

 i) Definition of objectives
 ii) Preparation of materials
 iii) Analysis of contribution from subject disciplines
 iv) Translation of scheme into practical terms, e.g. time allowance and staff allocation, for acceptance by trial schools.

(*b*) Possibly outline wider scheme of which the selected area might be a part.

All this to be done with, as far as possible, full teacher co-operation and discussion.

Stage IV

Trial in limited number of pilot schools, with feedback reports, teacher induction conferences and feedback conferences. Subsequent refinement and modification of materials.

Stage V

Wide trials of refined materials, perhaps concurrently with development of sample packs to illustrate other areas mentioned in Stage III. There might well not be time for this latter since, if one or two areas are to be worked on in detail, then different sections of those areas might need to be on trial.

Stage VI

Evaluation to answer questions:

1 How far does integrated course achieve its professed objectives and contribute more or better than a separate subject approach? What is left outside that is of value? What is the impact on children and what is their understanding of and reaction to it?

2 How far can an integrated approach provide intellectually reputable curricula?

3 What adjustments are desirable in school organization for maximum success of an integrated course, supposing that satisfactory answers are found to 1 and 2?

4 What new teaching techniques or learning situations are necessary or desirable?

5 Is integration more appropriate at any age range than at others?

6 Bearing in mind ultimate examination pressures, how can integrated schemes fade in to traditional syllabuses? Or should they?

7 How far is success related to the scope of integration? Or how all-embracing does integrated course need to be to be worthwhile?

N.B. At all stages the project must have regard to existing practice and organization of schools and the pressures they are subject to. If materials and schemes are to be tried out, they must be in a form in which the schools can accept them. The schools are not likely to change their organization radically until they are convinced that it is for a good purpose.

Comment

It is useful to compare this statement with the extracts from the original submission, quoted by Shipman on pp. 6–8, and with his analysis of what actually happened. It will be seen that this memorandum is, in some ways, closer to the latter than the former. This would suggest that we were influenced by it. I am sure we were, but I think it important to see this document as a perceptive clarification of the way things were developing rather than offering essentially new suggestions.

Linking it up with aspects of the project that will be discussed later, three points may be noted. It assumes without question that materials will be developed; it suggests questions for evaluation that lay beyond the time span or financial resources of the project; and it makes no mention whatever of diffusion.

Looking at its short-term effects, one can now see it offered us a tripwire. This comes in the second half of the first sentence: 'the statement of its advantages'. I think that a project must negotiate its trial schools on a different basis than that used to diffuse its ideas at a later stage. In appealing for trial schools, one can only invite them to join in an experiment. One just does not know whether the trials will prove or disprove 'advantages'. Only in the diffusion stage is one in any position to make claims. This is not to deny that some teachers pressed us for 'statements of advantages' (often, one guesses, to use as ammunition in their local war with colleagues or a head), but I think we were ill advised to offer what we did, as the next document may show.

(2) AGENDA FOR AN EXTRAORDINARY MEETING OF THE ADVISORY COMMITTEE (JULY 1968)

Circumstances

At the end of the first six months, the team produced a 'first-stage report'. This was a lengthy document, which summarized the work that coordinators had seen in schools, discussed definitions of 'integration' and the 'humanities', outlined the way ahead, and surveyed a possible range of themes and support materials.

It was arranged for this to be discussed at an enlarged meeting of the advisory Committee, lasting a full day. In addition to its regular members, all the team was invited to attend, as well as a number of local headmasters and representatives of examining boards. To focus the discussion, the following agenda was prepared. This summarizes the larger document, and in places, quotes from it.

Document: Agenda for discussion of first progress report

I   PROJECT ORGANIZATION AND CURRICULUM DEVELOPMENT WORK

Covered in sections one and two. Mainly informative, for general interest and in answer to a number of enquiries.

II INTEGRATED WORK IN SCHOOLS

Shows a wide variety of approaches, but some generalizations are possible:

(a) Most experiments are in the fourth and fifth form, and with the less able child.

(b) Most frequent themes are:
Study of the district
Topical issues
Vocational problems
Becoming adult

III DEFINITION OF 'INTEGRATION OF HUMANITIES' AND STATEMENT OF ADVANTAGES

Project faced with difficulties not shared by projects developing established school subjects:

(a) To define terms

(b) To justify possible inclusion of 'integrated humanities' in school curriculum

(1) DEFINITIONS: 'INTEGRATION': the exploration of theme, problem and area of enquiry, which requires help from more than one subject discipline, by the concerted action of a group of teachers. Extent and nature of 'concerted action' to be decided within each individual school.

'HUMANITIES': in general terms, those subjects or aspects of subjects which would 'help deepen a child's rational and imaginative understanding of the human situation'. In practice, the range of interest will largely be determined by the specialisms of the teachers involved, and a headmaster may well select teachers for their personal qualities, rather than to achieve a particular combination of subjects.

(2) JUSTIFICATION OF INTEGRATION OF THE HUMANITIES
Possible difficulties

(a) Require changes in school resources with heavier **expenditure** on library rather than textbooks.

(b) Movements of staff could badly disrupt a team teaching approach and agreed programme.

(c) Need to think out new methods of assessing pupil performance within school.

(d) Public examinations.

(e) Doubts of subject teachers.

Possible advantages

For pupils:

(a) A fuller exploration of themes either chosen by them or close to their life interests.

(b) Gives an extra significance to school subjects by enabling them to be seen as tools to tackle larger problems.

(c) Increases the capacity of the mind for more rigorous academic work.

(d) Could help ability of child to integrate experience meaningfully, in a way closer to life.

For teachers:

(a) Encourages increased participation from staff as a whole in curriculum planning.

(b) More support from colleagues and breakdown of teachers' isolation in classroom.

For headmaster:

(a) Potentially stimulates cooperation of staff and understanding of each other's subjects.

(b) Makes full use of staff, by giving scope to able teacher and support to weak one.

(c) Could help towards a more flexible timetable.

For society:

(a) Makes possible the discussion of large, complex and urgent social issues, which would not fit naturally into any subject area.

(b) Gives greater facility for inclusion of new knowledge and topical material.

IV STRATEGY OF PROJECT

   I SEQUENCE

     (a) Preparation of teaching material.

     (b) Initial trial of material (with concern for specific teaching problems).

     (c) Revision of material.

   2 THEMES

     Main areas:

     (a) The Human Life Cycle

     (b) Living in Society

     (c) The World Framework

     (d) The Human Condition

     (e) Value Problems

   3 MATERIAL KITS

     Containing:

     (a) Range of problem

     (b) List of available material

     (c) Materials themselves

     (d) Suggestions for use

Comment

Once again, comparisons are useful, especially with the statements from the project information sheets of 1970 and later, which Shipman quotes on pp. 8 and 19. In those documents one finds that the definitions of 'integration' and 'humanities' have remained constant. The decisions about materials units have sharpened, but are consistent with the first suggestions. One may also ask how far it reflects, or goes against, the Schools Council memo just discussed. Certainly the desired 'statement of advantages' can now be seen as no more than hopes and guesses. The problems of evaluation – although more fully discussed in the report – are not mentioned in the summary, nor were they in the meeting itself.

It happens to be the one meeting of which a transcript – in telegram language – exists. The team played a passive role, defending points when raised, but only asserting themselves on one issue:

upholding enquiry over against instruction. Very little was said by college of education lecturers, except on the issue of teacher training. The sole representative of the Schools Council mostly sat silently. Essentially the meeting was dominated by the headmasters, counterpointed by comments from the advisers.

Broadly, the heads were not interested in definitions – though some conflicting ones peeped through – nor in possible gains from integration. Indeed, they were more concerned with what was left out of the document than what was in it. The topics that aroused most discussion were:

1 *Team teaching* – apart from one ardent advocate ('one of the great advantages is that they really form a very self-critical evolving group') there was hesitation, and this was later to prove the aspect that was to arouse most apprehension in the negotiations with trial schools.

2 *Appropriate age groups* – a grammar school head said the focus must be on the first two years, while secondary modern heads wanted the stress on the fourth-form leaver. The project, in the report, had argued for working across the first five years. The Schools Council representative broke silence to comment: 'Integration different for first two years than last two years. Foresee difficulties in keeping these different varieties of people. Slow business, and better for it to be slow. If one embarks on two separate strategies one may have difficulties.'

3 *Examinations* – mainly about how many credits would it represent on a final certificate.

4 *Staffing and the timetable.*

The whole was spiced with criticisms of the report's 'high-sounding language', and descriptions of experiments in their own schools.

Commenting in the light of how things worked out later, three things strike me now:

(1) *The foolishness of being prematurely precise.* Projects are under understandable pressure by heads and advisers to say exactly what

will be involved – they want to know the limits of the threat represented by a project! I think this should be resisted. I find myself,
for example, in that meeting being pressed to answer that humanities work might represent ten periods a week of thirty-five minutes
each, whereas this was just the kind of point that was much more
satisfactorily negotiated separately with each school, during the
year that followed.

(2) *The waste of an opportunity.* What use, it was asked, should be
made of the report? The Schools Council was against its going to
teachers' centres. Heads thought the time for statements was much
later. So it was dropped. To me, this was doubly unfortunate. It
was depressing to the team, leaving the feeling that six months of
effort was not worth knowing about. More serious in the long run
(as will be discussed under diffusion) it was not used to start discussion among those interested across the country. There is a great
value in projects letting people hear them thinking aloud
Alone at that meeting some of the teachers saw the value in using
the report to stimulate discussions, and one of the diagrams used
appears – in that spirit – in the final version of the handbook
(SC15P 1972).

(3) *The development of curriculum units.* Little was said about the
suggested themes, apart from a query whether parents might be
upset. Nothing at all was said about materials. And yet, twenty
out of the twenty-nine pages of the report concerned with the
future had been devoted to themes and materials. There was a
problem implicit here, which now needs discussion.

'The materials madness'

All was not well with materials. Shipman has some sharp observations to make. These can be summarized as:

1 The production of materials for publication came to dominate
  the life of the project in a way that excluded other developments
  and increased the movement towards centralization.

2 The concentration on materials can partly be seen as an evasion of the less accessible problems of definition and research.

3 Materials were not the main thing asked for by either teachers or advisers.

4 Materials produced were regarded by the teachers as too difficult, and they found they needed to spend a considerable time modifying them.

5 The publication arrangements were a compromise, forced on us by time, which left the senior units unpublished.

6 Controversies over materials produced sharper tensions within the team than any other aspect of the project's work.

My first inclination would be to make a few modifications. I think it is vital to distinguish, for example, between the raw trial materials that teachers criticized, and the actual materials that were published, refined and modified in both content and format through those very criticisms. Again, I think there were differences in their attitude to materials between advisers and teachers. Teachers' criticisms arose out of their very concern to be supported by materials. There were also differences among the advisers themselves. The gravamen of one adviser's comments was not against producing materials, but that in giving large packs to trial schools we blocked their initiative and made teachers feel they must faithfully work through every sheet of paper. Another felt that teachers needed most help with the method, and thus he welcomed the publication of a handbook, rather than the packs. And so on.

Having made such modifications, however, I think the points stand, and they raise the central question of why things developed that way. Shipman, in analysing the complex of pressures that a project experiences, goes a long way to answer the question. There are two dimensions, however, he says little about, or where I see things differently: the one before he became a close observer of the project, and the other because he was not concerned with evaluating materials.

The first thing to assert is that material production was seen as a

central concern of the project from the start. It was not something
that emerged as a possible solution when we were struggling to define our procedures. The prevalent model for curriculum developers
at the time the project was founded was that of Nuffield Science,
and their materials had already begun their 'best seller' story.
'Resources for Learning' was the vogue phrase and the name of a
new Nuffield Project. The proposals submitted to the Schools
Council enshrine materials less in words than in the £5000 allocated
to their production out of the total budget of £29,000. I myself
only yielded to persuasions to be the Director on the promise that
the project would primarily be concerned with experimenting with
materials. When team members were appointed, their potential
contribution to published materials was taken into account. Before
the project began, the Nuffield Schools Council Humanities Project,
whose director was on our advisory committee, had announced the
themes for which they would be developing support materials.
One of the seminal statements for us – as for many people working
in the humanities field – was Bruner's *Man: A Course of Study*, with
its stimulating (and expensive) suggestions for learning through
materials. Already, by March 1968 – three months after the project
began – at the first public meeting where I spoke about the project,
I was thinking aloud about themes and materials. Coordinators, as
part of their first visits to schools, were asked to record the themes
they found in schools, and ask for new ideas for units supported by
materials. And, as already noted, these dominate the first stage report of July of that year.

However, to say that we had a central interest in materials from
the start is not the same as saying we wanted them to dominate, as
they came to. Somehow, the whole thing gathered speed and got
out of hand. One can now see danger signals, even in the early days.
There is the precipitate listing of themes, almost before asking about
integrated studies. The question of whether material was, or was
not, the way forward was never openly discussed in the team –
although one member informally raised doubts. Yet at least one
contemporary project challenged the prevailing orthodoxy. The

Environmental Studies Project, for instance, concentrated on the analysis of detailed profiles of work in schools to draw out guidelines for teachers, and these now form the core of their publications. Once committed, as we were, to materials, their importance proliferated, not least because they were found to involve more work than we ever realized. One can also see the force of the process detected by Shipman: they are more clear-cut to concentrate on than intractable problems of definition. A commitment, then, there from the start had – for a number of reasons – gained uncomfortable momentum.

Yet all this, it seems to me, is only half the story. The complementary and more positive consideration is that materials, structured to support the exploration of large themes, were fundamental to our whole approach to integrated studies. I don't think Shipman would dissent from this; it simply lay outside his area of concern. To provide a balance, however, some comments are needed here. The development of materials, as we saw it, cannot be separated from considerations of teaching strategy and of an ideas framework, which is why all our published materials are accompanied by a teachers' guide, which looks at both these aspects. Prior to any search for or selection of materials, was a concern to justify the theme itself and to analyse the range of issues that comprised it.

Putting the stress as we did on an enquiry approach, with subjects as distinctive tools, materials became important as raw evidence. Through the handling of this evidence, subject skills may be trained and insights gained. Different subjects may be concerned with different types of evidence, or may approach the same evidence with a different strategy. We became caught with the idea that integrated studies may thus involve the multi-use of the same materials – to some it may be data to be analysed, for others stimulus for imaginative exploration. A detailed diagram showing a range of approaches to a work of art, for example, was included in the first stage report, and is to be published in a history symposium. It may be added that 'materials' was always widely interpreted: artefacts were treasured as well as texts, picked-up objects as well as pictures. We encouraged

– as many schools had long done – the environment as a resource. Thus our enthusiasm for materials was never limited to what could be published. And we insisted that our published materials started but did not cover an enquiry – both teachers and pupils would contribute others as their own enquiry took its own route.

Materials, then, were the most visible expression of, and were inseparable from, our double concern:

(a) the exploration of important human themes
(b) by an enquiry approach, drawing on a range of subject skills and ideas

If one lined up the three components here – materials development, analysis of the content of the curriculum, research into enquiry methods – and considered the degree of project time and resources spent on them, then it may be significant that the proportions would reflect the emphases of the Schools Council at that time. We gave most to materials, and in this the Schools Council fully supported us. We gave rather less to analyses of classroom procedures. The Schools Council checked our plans in this area by refusing funds for evaluation. Also, looked at more widely, the Council needed (to cite a project proposal submitted to them in 1971) to do far more in analysing and reviewing teaching methods that are common to a range of projects. Projects tend to search alone, and, at the end of the day, hawk their wares alone – if not in competition. As for the content of the curriculum, it is not that we did not give a good deal of thought to this, but rather that our efforts are marked by significant withdrawal. Up to the selection of six themes for development we had schemes, which looked at the whole range of work in the humanities; afterwards there was instead a lot of time spent justifying our themes, arguing that they made a 'total package', or showing where they could be slotted into existing school timetables. Understandable enough, but giving little help to the underlying concern that was to come through at most meetings during the 'diffusion' year: What are we teaching in schools?

Why? And what does it all add up to? The origins of the Schools Council forbade it to look at the whole curriculum, but the work of an individual project was restricted without it.

Before leaving a consideration of materials and the process of innovation, two further issues need to be touched on – the role of publishers, and the significance of materials in diffusion. The publishing issue is discussed in the following pages. Little needs to be added here. Perhaps we should stress that those comments apply primarily to our experience, and that there was among Schools

Figure 7

Council projects the greatest variety of styles of relationship with publishers, as indeed of end-product – ranging through course books, kits, journals, teachers' guides, multi-copies of resource items – and the situation is commented on in Sturdy (1972). Also, one might add that the short life of projects tends to defeat a desirable timetable for publication. Teachers, for example, were so preoccupied during the first trial year with organizational issues that they were just not in a position to reflect on and report back on materials. Later, teachers began to feel freer to do this, but already we had had to start revising them for publication. Even then, materials were not published until eight months after the team had disbanded, and so were not there to help in their diffusion.

As for this issue of materials and diffusion – to lead into the next section – a simple piece of didacticism is shown in Figure 7 to set the scene.

If one looks at the five aspects of change in Figure 7, three points can be baldly made: it is impossible to change any one of them without producing need for changes in the others; it is far easier – dangerously so – to introduce new materials than it is to modify the rest, which become progressively more resistant to change; hence, new materials can be completely frustrated by an inadequate response in the other areas. So – as angry letters in *Dialogue* and *The Times Educational Supplement* have suggested – at the very least one should not sell materials without training teachers in their use. Unfortunately, you also need very much more.

And leave not a pack behind

The fear of projects is that their cloud-capped towers will disappear into thin air, and leave no trace on the educational landscape. Shipman offers a chapter on how far integrated studies remained in former trial schools after the end of the project. The desire, however, went wider than that. We hoped that integrated studies would be taken up by schools in many parts of the country, and that integrated studies would become an accepted constituent of the system. Our project was local and short lived. Would the work become national and permanent? What remains to discuss is not whether this has happened – it certainly has not – but what steps were taken to help it come about.

A useful framework for looking at this aspect is that defined in Hoyle (1972), although in places it will need adaptation as his focus is on a school as the unit. He summarizes his Research, Development and Dissemination (RD & D) model of innovation as shown on

p. 160. He adds the comment – which reflects our experience – that:
It can be argued that the present state of affairs in Britain is as follows. New agencies of *research* and *development* have been created in recent years and there is considerable focus on these stages. These new agencies are developing strategies of *demonstration* and *dissemination* and agencies of dissemination which

existed previously are developing new strategies. However, the agencies concerned have not hitherto been greatly concerned with the processes of *implementation* and *institutionalization*, and specialized agencies for these tasks have not yet emerged.

Stage	Function
Research	To provide the knowledge basis for innovation.
Development	To produce the innovation.
Dissemination	To inform potential adopters about an innovation.
Demonstration	To gain the acceptance of an innovation by potential users through demonstrating its effectiveness.
Implementation	To incorporate the innovation into a school.
Institutionalization	To ensure that the innovation becomes a fully functioning and relatively permanent part of the school.

(I) RESEARCH AND DEVELOPMENT STAGES

If one looks at these with the needs of the later stages in mind, then one is made more sharply aware that the Keele project was too short. There was far more research needed before one could possibly give all the informed guidance likely to be asked by schools considering the adoption of integrated studies. Only two years of trial, for example, were possible, whereas one needed to follow through a pupil's performance in integrated studies across a secondary school career, including his performance in public examinations.

Indeed, the problem is more basic. At the end of the project a memo was sent to the Schools Council commenting on our experiences, and it will give a working edge to this concluding discussion if sections of it are quoted at length. On the immediate point, two things were stressed:

(a) *The restricted nature of the research so far undertaken*
There is little more to offer than the advice in the introductory handbook. No member of the team had any previous experience of evaluation, nor was any money allowed for this in the original estimate. The general observation and recording of experiences was, in fact, an extra demand on the co-ordinators, over and above what was originally envisaged for them – and some of them were already under considerable pressure because of the unforeseen amount of work involved in materials production. The request for an additional member with a training in measurement techniques was refused.

In these circumstances, the project only claims to have made itself aware of the range of factors involved in integrated studies, but not to have studied any of them in depth and detail.

(b) *The necessity of continuous research*
So many of the questions asked by teachers really press back on areas of research not yet undertaken, e.g. questions about: *pupil achievement and assessment* (Skills involved? Nature of learning process? Sequence? Appreciating interrelationship?); *organization* (Pattern of school community?); *content of integrated studies* (Nature of knowledge? Total school curriculum?).

The fundamental danger for integrated studies is that development at the shop-floor level will be built on too slender a research base.

(2) DISSEMINATION AND DEMONSTRATION
These are the stages covered by the word 'diffusion', as it is now generally used. In the event, the only action taken by the project

G

was by one person. The Schools Council funded me for a further twelve months, after the team had been disbanded in July 1971.

The memorandum already quoted has a good deal to say about 'diffusion', and the feeling of the team, reinforced by my experience the year later, was that more should have been done *from early on* – a point touched on when discussing the first stage report. In commenting on what could have been done during the main life of the project, the 1972 memo read as follows:

In retrospect, it can be seen that two essential tasks were only partially achieved. In some measure, this was because their significance was not fully recognized. But it was also because money (and hence time and labour of team members) was not available. In turn, this was because the cost of diffusion was not built in to the original project budget – a weakness of nearly all projects launched at that time. The two failure areas were:

(a) *The training of teachers involved in the project*
Far more is meant here than familiarizing teachers with what was expected of them during trials. Ideally, at the end of the project, there should have been a body of teachers with an understanding of curriculum development and a firm grasp of the ideas and approaches to integrated studies. There would thus have been a resource of trained manpower who could have played a fundamental role in diffusion.

This is not to deny that teachers came out of trials with a fund of practical experience, and one is very grateful for the help several have given in talking at meetings, but the project failed to leave behind a body of articulate teachers in the sense that the North West Regional Curriculum Development Project did, after the special insistence of Dr Rudd to initiate teachers into curriculum thinking.

(b) *Nationwide network of critical friends*
Throughout the project, letters of enquiry were answered

with a brief handout, and requests to speak were honoured, but it was a marginal concern.

Ideally, *from the start*, there should have been such features as: Regular newsletter.

Critical discussion forums with specialized groups (e.g. LEA advisers, subject specialists, college lecturers), invited from outside the project area.

Close liaison with teachers' centres (e.g. using some of them for pilot working parties on aspects of integration).

Through such methods a range of interested individuals and groups would have been developed, who would have formed the growth points of later diffusion.

The same memo then turned to consider how these two approaches would have provided a basis for diffusion in the closing months, and after the end of the project:

> What this stage must do is develop more fully aspects (*a*) and (*b*) mentioned above – the *local resource* and the *nationwide network*. By the end of this stage every interested person should have been in a position to obtain detailed information about the project's work and ideas – and even more, the chance to discuss these with people (team members/teachers) who had been involved in it. Materials need to be published before the team disbands, so that they can be scrutinized alongside these talks and discussions. And a number of schools, teachers' centres and LEAs should have launched on a development programme, implementing – or at least experimenting with – integrated studies. In doing so, one key aid and reference point should be the schools and LEAs in which the project worked. How far did all this actually happen?

A. THE LOCAL RESOURCE

By the end of the project, with schools and LEAs, two things were happening:

(*a*) Some advisers/teachers were feeling that they had given considerable help to the project, and now they wished to withdraw, not have visitors, etc.

(b) Personnel had changed/were changing – moved to other areas – and thus caused discontinuity with trial work, or at least broke the link with Keele.

Such developments were natural, and partly unavoidable. Moreover, they should be set against two other factors:

(a) A nucleus of former trial schools continued to (and still do) welcome visitors.

(b) Nearly all former trial schools have continued with integrated studies, even if with modifications.

Yet, on balance, it must be admitted that the schools have not played as central a role in diffusion as could have been the case. Two general themes seem to call for further exploration by LEAs, Schools Council, etc.:

1 *Continuity of commitment*

To agree to help an experiment during the lifetime of a project is not enough. Both from the viewpoint of a 'return for investment', as well as from the long-term survival of the development area in question, a longer commitment by LEA/school seems essential. This may be worth spelling out at the start of a project. It may also mean that the Schools Council may have to think more in terms of some 'continuity service' after the end of a project.

2 *Deployment of former team members*

There seems to be a tremendous wastage of experience at the end of a project. A group of people, with almost unique experience in an area of curriculum development, get sucked back haphazardly into 'the system', instead of their becoming key people in project diffusion.

B. THE NATIONWIDE NETWORK

As said, this aspect of diffusion partly depends on exploiting the contacts of 'critical friends' which should have been built up from the start. In our case, it was launched by two national conferences, at Keele and Sussex, during the last fortnight of the full team. During the course of the extra year for the Director, contacts were made with, and meetings held at university institutes of education, colleges of education, LEAs and teachers' centres. As far as they went, they were probably useful, but:

(a) The *national coverage* was *haphazard*.

(b) *Limited part* was taken by *trial school teachers* (partly for reasons mentioned above, partly from difficulty of release during school hours, partly because one LEA refused).

(c) *Too short* (a single meeting, or even a weekend conference, is not a satisfactory alternative to the week-long training operations undertaken by the Nuffield Schools Council Humanities Project, with its fuller resources).

Looking back, these comments now seem too much a kicking against might-have-beens, and unfair to two sources of support received during the year, both of which may represent growth points. On the one hand, there was the Schools Council itself. Their information centre and publicity services, the use of their London headquarters for open days, the support of the field officers, with their national coverage, all helped. During the year, the Council arranged a series of conferences with teachers' centre leaders across the country and project diffusion was one of the key issues. Too late to help us, but important, a committee was established to look at diffusion, and it became recognized that diffusion should be a component in the funding of all future projects. On the other hand, there were the publishers, the Oxford University Press. From early on, they recognized that they were not just marketing materials, but were also helping develop a new approach, involving changes in methods and syllabuses. They organized exhibitions and talks – especially at teachers' centres, and the editor herself gave a number of lectures on the ideas behind the project. And they will be issuing a six-monthly bulletin, reporting on the experiences of schools using the material, as well as giving up-to-date information about books, articles and examination syllabuses on integrated studies.

The disturbing thing is, judging by enquiries, that the work needed to be done during these stages is far from done, but any support can only now be given on top of other full-time jobs, and without secretarial and other resources. Once again, it is with a sense of 'job unfinished' that one turns to the next stages.

(3) IMPLEMENTATION AND INSTITUTIONALIZATION

These stages go beyond 'diffusion' as generally understood. Although one could turn to individual schools to illustrate the process, one could not turn to any planned operation, supported by the Schools Council, which can be seen as a direct continuation of the project. Whatever launching power the project had is now spent. If integrated studies is going to be institutionalized within individual schools, this will ultimately depend on the support of existing and more permanent institutions outside those schools. Some of them are mentioned in the following chapter: LEAs, training organizations, examination boards and professional bodies, as well as those concerned with research. The most formidable task, the most costly and the least considered, lies ahead.

And there an end, except perhaps to glance at two strands, which grow out of the foregoing and unexpectedly take us back to the very start of the project. Both spring from the needs of schools who wish to experiment with integrated studies. On the one hand, they will need to be able to turn to somebody, or some body that can give them the kind of support not dissimilar to that given by the project when it was available to trial schools when they launched into integrated studies. On the other hand, teachers will be aware of gaps in their knowledge and of the unfamiliarity of the process and hence feel the need of courses or some form of training, just as the long-term continuity of integrated studies also goes back to the training of teachers.

The desire for a permanent support body has often been expressed. In one sense, this need is met by the advisers and the teachers' centres within an authority. But their resources are spread so wide that they may not be able to give any precise or sustained support to integrated studies. Similarly, the Schools Council has so wide a range of projects that it cannot be expected, in any detailed way, to be responsible for their after-care. It has, however, had a system of subject committees with a watching brief on developments, and some such oversight could be given to integrated studies. Also, this need for nurturing growth points from projects might be better handled by the regionalization of the Schools Council – to pick up the fruitful idea of Morrell, mentioned in Shipman's first chapter. Another possibility discussed has been the founding of an association for integrated studies, analogous to those in other subject areas – holding conferences, publishing a journal, etc. There has been some tendency to react, 'Not another!' At the same time, the project clearly missed out on the kind of important support the General Studies Association gave to the York project, and which will now give continuity to its work and ideas.

No outside support, however, is more fundamental than the opportunity for training, whether for teachers on the job, or in preparation for the profession. The 'Schools Council' tag perhaps leads one to overlook the fact that the working context throughout was an area training organization – the Keele Institute of Education. As already seen, the proposal for a teachers' centre – first put forward as the project was about to start – can only be understood in a general strategy of seeing in-service training as a permanent agent of curriculum change. College lecturers were members of the advisory committee throughout, helped with materials and courses, and took part in the observers' panel, which reviewed the project's work. Curriculum study itself – as a new area of study – was brought into the Institute through a course run by the team. From midway in the project, a proposal was put forward to the Department of Education and Science for a three-year project, based on the colleges within the Keele area, to review how innovations from projects in the humanities area (not least integrated studies) called for changes in the training of teachers. One may suggest that the rebuff to this proposal may have owed something to the unfortunate demarcation between the Schools Council and the DES – developments in schools concerning the former, in colleges the latter, whereas every innovation in schools called out for changes in colleges. Again, stimulated not least by the presence of the project, the local college of education at Madeley has developed a department for curriculum study. They have gained a close knowledge of three projects in the humanities field: the Humanities Curriculum Project, the Bruner *Man: A Course of Study*, and Keele Integrated Studies. They have full documentation, and the published materials from all of them. Curriculum study forms part of the course for all their students in training, and they have made some experiments with training students for team teaching. Lecturers from other colleges visit them to discuss the introduction of something similar themselves. Lastly, a recent reorganization of courses for Advanced Diplomas in Education, aimed to make them both more specialist and more practically orientated, includes two that are interdisciplinary – one in General Studies and one in World Studies. It would be unfair to claim that the project alone was responsible for all these growth points, but it would be even more unfair not to recognize that a project may be a catalyst for change in its host institution, and in being so, it may stimulate developments that will support its work after the team has scattered.

9. Implications

To generalize from one project in thirty-eight schools would be to compound the current superstructure of curriculum theory that has risen on an unfortunately meagre base. The list that follows has been derived from the evidence as I saw it. Readers will appreciate from Chapters 6 and 8 that there are other perspectives. Furthermore, this is not merely an insider/outsider view. Bolam and Jenkins interpret some aspects of the organization of the project differently. Similarly Jenkins exposes the different views among teachers, and such internal contrasts were also apparent inside the agencies contrasted in Chapter 3.

Integrated studies

This study was not concerned to evaluate integrated studies. But integration is now popular, and many of the problems that overtook the Keele project were caused by the under-estimation of the difficulties involved. The project team tried hard to spell these out, but schools still tried to integrate without establishing in advance what was to be integrated and how it was to be done.

(a) DEFINING THE INNOVATION
Integration could be attempted at the level of children, subjects, teachers, and even schools. At each level there are many approaches.

The Keele approach was to try to encourage integration through team teaching by subject specialists working at common themes. Few schools, however, implemented this version. Most went for integrated teachers. Others saw integration as a way of breaking down divisions between children in different streams, as a way of creating a relevant, unspecialized curriculum or as a link between primary and secondary schools. Even when the style of integration was similar, the emphasis on team teaching or learner-centred methods or the use of resources differed. Things may be easier when the innovation is in a single subject area. But definitions made outside schools are unlikely to coincide with those negotiated within. Similarly the definitions of advisers, inspectors, teachers' centre wardens, Schools Council field officers are likely to vary. Wasnedge (1971) has suggested that projects may disappear almost without trace. It is also likely that if and when they were traced, the version being practised would be unrecognizable to those who originally promoted it. Consequently, the researcher looking for residues must be prepared to dig deep and not to rely on first impressions.

(b) RESISTANCE TO INTEGRATION

A popular assumption of many theorists of the curriculum is that teachers stoutly defend the boundaries of their specialist subjects against marauding pedlars of integration. Subjects are seen as genuine disciplines accounting for the strength of the resistance to change. But the subject is seen as giving not only security and meaning in an often hostile world but also the prestige and rewards which are threatened along with promotion prospects by involvement in integration. In the schools studied here, largely secondary moderns, this rarely applied. The teachers not only accepted integration but often pressed, beyond the specialist version outlined in project documents, to become generalists. It may be that social scientists, specialists themselves, educated in selective schools and universities, have taken the minority of graduate specialists as typical of the teaching profession. If the tide towards integration grows stronger the difficulty may be to retain subject disciplines rather than to break them down.

(c) INTEGRATION AND AUTHORITY

Lortie (1969), Bernstein (1967 and 1973) and Musgrove (1973) have argued that integration, team teaching and learner-centred methods will alter the authority structure of the school. But for every argument that these will increase the power of the head there are others saying it will hand over power to the teachers. The key seems to lie in the visibility of integrated methods. But there was no evidence in the schools studied here that this led to increased power to the head. All these hunches about schools are over-generalizations. Ignoring the complexities of staff organization, there were heads who had to be reminded that an experiment in integration was going on in their schools. There were others deeply and, as it turned out, harmfully, involved in the innovation. Powerful faculties had formed in some schools but in others integration seemed to have given the head oversight of the teachers involved. The level of generality in these theoretical papers is too high. The diversity is too great for such theories before at least some categorization of schools has been made.

Curriculum innovation in schools

It helps to think of schools as social systems, even if it doesn't explain anything. The advantage is that innovation in one part is expected to create change throughout as the system adjusts. In practice the main impact was on the innovating teachers as they felt the strain of doing something new amid a fixed routine. In other subject areas there was rarely much effect from the introduction of integrated studies. But those involved nevertheless felt exposed, vulnerable and overworked when they compared their position with that of the rest of the staff.

(*a*) DIVERGENT INNOVATION

Throughout this book there has been a continuing stress on the unpredictable outcome of a clearly defined innovation. It was only through probing at interviews that the way a school had developed from the initial commitment could be detected. Much had disappeared but a lot had been used in new courses, new methods and new organization. The project had acted as a catalyst, speeding up change in many schools. In some the catalyst slowed it down or even stopped it. This accelerating or decelerating effect was more common than development along project lines. The investment from outside had given some schools a fillip towards integration. Even those teachers who finally rejected the approach of the project had been forced to think out their own role in the context of the innovation.

(*b*) COUNTER-INNOVATION

The slow rate of curriculum change is usually associated with the conservatism of teachers, or, in more sophisticated analyses, the constraints exercised within the school and classroom situation. There may, however, be a very good reason for resisting innovation. Throughout this project worry over standards of work persisted. This was no mere excuse for inaction but a genuine concern for the children, which was again prominent when teachers looked back over the years of trial. The Keele team was close enough to its trial schools to realize this. To more distant teams it would have looked like conservatism.

This assessment of innovation against the learning of children was encouraging, for it is the ultimate criterion. The variety of outcomes of the Keele project included many that seemed to violate the principles laid down by the team. But whether integration was given up or changed to a homespun type, the rejection of the project model, and particularly the substitution of another, was still a positive response. The schools on which the project had the most effect were often those that had rejected it most forcibly. The critical teachers and their contrary views on integration were often those who had moved furthest as a result of participation, even though the direction in which they had gone was not that intended at Keele.

(c) PRIVACY AND PUBLICITY
Innovation involves exposure within the school and to visitors from outside. The teachers both disliked and appreciated this attention. Innovation can founder on this ambivalence but can also feed off it. The Keele project, because it was close to the schools and had local coordinators, was able to give a lot of attention. Five schools did take off towards self-sustained innovation. But local supporting agencies such as teachers' centres were only available in one area and without these even publicity through discussion with fellow teachers was difficult. Most schools felt that there had been little reward for much effort, and consequently remained shy of the lime-light. In the worst cases they felt like zoo animals, peered at by visitors interested in the project rather than them. But most teachers had come to welcome visitors and the chance to give their views. Lasting curriculum innovation may depend on mobilizing this desire for recognition. Given the competence of many trial school teachers who spoke at meetings and diffusion conferences of this project, there would be a lot to gain.

(d) THE SCHOOL CONTEXT FOR INNOVATION
The trial schools that implemented some form of team teaching and learner-centred activity as well as integrating subjects had a major upheaval in their midst. Surprisingly, even with a team of six or more the innovation was not necessarily seen as the concern of the remainder of the staff. The integrated studies team seemed to be operating without anyone else being particularly concerned. But the strain was felt within the team. Everything they did was more visible, more active than usual, and was often an inconvenience to others. Yet even in schools where there was more than one curriculum innovation there had been no attempt to plan on a school-wide

basis. At the end of the project two schools had decided that this school-wide planning was necessary, but this was the result of experience not foresight.

The organization of curriculum development projects

Much has been said already about the way curriculum projects could be organized for maximum effect. Many of the changes recommended would produce a very different project organization and style from that described here, although the strong local links were important pointers. Meanwhile, thinking at the Schools Council based on experience so far has produced some very different second-phase projects. But three points remain to be stressed if the more conventional type of project is to make the maximum impact. All are closely related.

(a) THE ESTABLISHMENT OF AN INFRASTRUCTURE

The Keele project and the parallel early Schools Council projects operated in the spaces between national and local agencies responsible for the schools. There was no organization they could have joined at the start or which could have carried on their work at the end. There was nothing that could pull together all the available educational services and all the current work in curriculum development. The teachers' centres are a move in the right direction, and the expansion of in-service training should help. But Morrell's early idea of local and regional centres for development remains to be implemented, except in the North West.

(b) THE COORDINATION OF LOCAL AND NATIONAL EFFORT

Nothing was more frustrating in the research into the Keele project than the difficulties encountered when local authority boundaries had to be crossed by coordinators, teachers, advisers and college of education lecturers. The officers of the Schools Council were seen as interlopers by local authority staff. The university was seen from the schools as both distant and irrelevant. Inadvertently, university, schools, local authorities, colleges of education and the various Schools Council projects and officers frustrated one another. All knew this was happening and realized its stupidity. An infrastructure for curriculum development could cure this, but equally could be killed by the suspicion. Behind Jenkins's guiding metaphors in Chapter 6 lies too much insulation between teachers and those outside the school.

(c) THE NEED FOR MORE TIME
The project that is funded for three years, even though it is likely to get an extension of another year, is still too short-lived to be efficient. Bolam, the Project Director, discusses this on p. 160. Hartley, one of the coordinators, commented on this book:

> I would certainly emphasize more strongly the time factor. Had we been given, say, five years, the following benefits could have accrued:
> (a) More time to define team thinking on objectives, eliminating some of the early woolly thought and over-elaborate policy documents.
> (b) There could have been a short, restricted feasibility study in a few select schools before the major trial began. This would have eventually saved time and given valuable experience.
> (c) There could have been a much better diffusion campaign.

Above all, the extra time could be used to ensure that the skills built up during the early life of projects were employed to greater effect. These skills tend to become effective just as the three-year project comes to an end. Once an infrastructure was organized there would be a chance for them to be used in the right place, with the right people. Meanwhile, unless the primary aim is only to develop new curriculum materials, projects should be planned over longer periods with more local participation. This would provide room for such approaches as Hartley's commando operations recommended on p. 93. The Keele project had the right organization, but too little time to establish a lasting support and diffusion service.

The wider context for innovation

The most alarming aspect of this study was the differing perspectives of those involved. This made evaluation difficult, for success for one party could be failure for another. There were, however, two reasons why this, or any other innovation, was likely to have a limited impact. First, there was a paradox. Innovation was choked by change, particularly school reorganization and turnover in personnel. Advisory staff, Schools Council officers, university and project team, trial school teachers, and advisory committee members, all changed across the life of the innovation. The consequent lack of continuity resulted in an uneven advance and, in some schools, an abrupt halt. The greater the change in the context of innovation, the less chance there seemed to be of success. But each innovation forms the context for the rest and the whole process could become self-defeating.

Behind the second reason for unprofitable innovation lay a dilemma. Only the teachers in the classroom can implement changes in curriculum. But every change in routine is a threat to teacher-pupil relations and to standards of work. As the attempt to accelerate change has led to curriculum projects being financed and organized outside the schools, there is every incentive for the teachers to be critical and to frustrate the innovators. The research problem is to sort out the difference between rejection as a defence against imposed change and rejection as a defence of standards of work. Because our means of measuring the impact of innovations on attainment are so crude, there is no easy way of sorting out these motives.

There is, however, a deeper worry. Every innovation requires more skill from teachers than conventional subject-based class teaching. The pioneers and the enthusiasts they attract can make the innovation work, can produce the results that make early evaluations positive, and can serve as a seed bed for its spread elsewhere. But the spread of an innovation involves increasing numbers of teachers who lack the skills and the enthusiasm of the pioneers. The promotion prospects of involvement in an innovation are also rapidly exhausted and the ambitious soon look to the next bandwagon. The result is that an apparently successful innovation in the hands of a few can fail when generally adopted and diluted. Many teachers may lack the skills necessary for integrated, learner-centred, open planned, team teaching strategies and would be more effective and happy with conventional teaching.

This final chapter was written after the author had moved from the University of Keele to work for a local authority. This proved to be a different world, yet local authorities and the university were important agencies in this and most innovations. The schools are yet another world. This is the context of curriculum innovation. The Keele project team, as with most curriculum developers, did its best in the spaces between these worlds, while appearing alien from each. The way to effective curriculum development may lie, not in more efficient projects, but in narrowing the distance between schools and the agencies in education that administer, advise and train, or generate new ideas. Such an education system might not even need development projects.

Appendix:
The collection of data

The methods used to collect information on the Keele Integrated Studies Project were determined by dual objectives. The first was to trace the origins, organization and implementation of the project. The second was to investigate the organization of the trial schools and the relation between this organization and that of the project. It was first necessary to find out how decisions were made within the project, how these were translated into programmes for action in schools, and then to investigate the impact of these actions on the schools and also the action of the schools on the implementation of integrated studies. The early days of the investigation showed that the project did not consist merely of a team of curriculum developers and of teachers in the schools. It became necessary to find out what influence was being exerted by all the parties, at both national and local level, who were exerting influence, whether as part of the advisory structure of the project or indirectly through their influence on one another.

The first objective necessitated an intimate knowledge of the working of the project as it developed. This had to include the relations between the Schools Council, the University of Keele, the local authority advisers and the publishers of material, as well as the project team. From September 1969 to August 1971, the author observed most of the meetings of the project team, the meetings of the project advisory committee, and of the observers' panel set up for evaluation. The author acted as a detached observer at these meetings, taking notes and only participating on the rare occasions when his advice was asked.

All the minutes of meetings and committees at Keele were made available. The Schools Council released the relevant papers of committees discussing this project. The project team gave open access to all documents and feedback. The obervers' panel, set up to evaluate the work of the project in the schools, provided copies of its reports.

This observational and documentary evidence was supplemented by an interviewing programme at the end of the project in 1971. All the key personnel in and around the project were interviewed, using a standard interviewing schedule and a tape recorder. These interviews covered the Schools Council personnel at the centre and in the field, the local authority advisers and key persons on the observers' panel and advisory committee. These taped interviews and the mass of documentary material that was made available were the pieces from which the jigsaw of the development of this project was built up. No single source would have been adequate. As the interviewing programme progressed it was possible to add questions to the standard schedule to find out why certain decisions had been made. Only by interviewing the various parties who saw the project from different viewpoints could a full picture be built up.

The second half of the research concentrated on the trial schools. In 1969 and early 1970, five of these were visited and discussions were held with the staff. From these discussions the problems that faced the innovating teacher were extracted and used as the basis for further work. During the same period in the first months of trial, data was collected by the project team and used to build up school profiles. The four project coordinators collected further information from the schools to add to the profiles, providing the indices of organization that were used as a basis for hunches and predictions.

The observations in schools continued through 1969 to 1971. Meetings at Keele, at teachers' centres and at schools organized within local authority areas were attended. Throughout this period the project was receiving feedback from the schools and collecting more through its coordinators. In the autumn of 1971 thirty-four of the thirty-eight schools that had at some time been in the trial were visited. One of the remaining schools refused to cooperate, and of the remaining three one had lost all the staff who had been involved and the other two had never been involved in any real sense in the project and sufficient information had already been collected on them.

Interviewing was carried out in the thirty-four schools. There was no attempt to interview a random sample of teachers. The object was to interview the teacher or teachers who had been most responsible for the project and the headteacher where he or she had played an active part. Thirty-five teachers and fourteen headteachers were interviewed using a structured schedule based on the earlier discussions with teachers. In many schools the teachers interviewed mentioned other teachers who they saw as also having played a crucial part but who were absent. The questionnaire used in the interviews was left to be filled in by these cases, and twenty-three were returned. It is not possible to even estimate a response rate and the data on these questionnaires was not used in the final calculations.

These methods were extremely crude. Furthermore, the indices that follow are also very inadequate. There were, however, four checks on reliability. First, it was possible to check the data obtained from the interviews against those collected during visits by the author and by the project team. Second, the questionnaires sent through the post from schools were used to check data from interviews. Third, documentary evidence was used to check against the opinions of those interviewed. Fourth, this was a follow-through study, stretching over three years. Hunches could easily be checked. It was not a single photograph, but a jigsaw built up over time. Each piece could be fitted into the total picture. The final check was provided by the existence of information collected by the independent observers' panel and by other researchers. Two of these provided valuable accounts of specific aspects of the work (Archer 1971, Jenkins 1972).

The definitions, indices and measures that were used, and the times when these were collected, were as follows.

Definitions, indices and techniques of data collection

OUTPUT

1. *The extent of innovation*
   (a) *Contractual success* was defined as the fulfilment by the school of 'contract' to try out integrated studies. Of thirty-eight schools twenty-two were, in this contractual sense, successes, seven were failures and five only entered as replacements in the second year of trial. Another four schools did not complete the trial period but left to continue with their version of integrated studies independent of the project. They were contractual failures although they were continuing with the innovation.
   (b) *Curriculum impact* was defined as the extent to which curriculum change had resulted from the trial experience. Each school was ranked on one of four three-point scales. These measured the amount of trial material in use after the end of the trial period, developments arising from the trial in integrated studies, developments in related fields of the humanities, and the persistence of forms of team teaching.

INPUT

2. *Investment by teachers and schools*
   (a) *Time and energy* invested by teachers was measured on three three-point scales. These covered attendance at meetings, accumulation of supplementary materials and the provision of feedback to the project.
   (b) *Investment by the school* was measured on another three-point scale covering the provision of a special team leader, adjustments to the timetable and the provision of special planning time for the team.

(c) *High-level manpower* was measured by the extent to which head, deputy head or heads and heads of departments were involved in teaching integrated studies.

(d) *Material resources* were measured by the provision and suitability of rooms and the availability of money and special facilities for the trial within the schools.

3. *The context for investment*

(a) *The basis for integrated studies* was assessed by the existence on the school curriculum of ongoing work before the trial in this or similar areas of the humanities.

(b) *The climate of innovation* was a subjective assessment by the central project team of the esprit in the schools on a scale derived from the OCDQ Form IV, Part III, developed by Halpin (1966).

References

ARCHER, R. G. (1971) *An interpretative analysis of the implications for teacher training perceived from teachers involved in trial schools of the Keele Integrated Studies Project*. Advanced Diploma Dissertation, University of Keele.

BANKS, L. J. (1969) 'Curriculum development in Britain, 1963-8'. *Journal of Curriculum Studies*, Vol. 1, No. 3, pp. 247-59.

BERNSTEIN, B. (1967) 'Open school, open society'. *New Society*, September, pp. 350-3.

BERNSTEIN, B. (1973) 'On the classification and framing of educational knowledge'. In BROWN, R. (ed.) *Knowledge, Education and Cultural Change*. London, Tavistock.

BLOOM, B. S. (1956) *Taxonomy of Educational Objectives, Handbook 1: Cognitive Domain*. New York, McKay.

BOLAM, D. (1971) 'Integrating the curriculum: a case study in the humanities'. *Paedagogica Europaea*, pp. 157-71.

BOLAM, D. (1972) 'The Keele Integrated Studies Project: four footnotes'. *General Education*, Spring, pp. 14-18.

BOLAM, D. (1973) 'Teamwork to launch teamwork'. *IDEAS*, No. 24, January, pp. 16-25.

CASTON, G. (1971) 'The Schools Council in context'. *Journal of Curriculum Studies*, Vol. 3, No. 1, pp. 50-64.

FESTINGER, L., RIECKEN, H. W., and SCHACHTER, S. (1956) *When Prophecy Fails*. University of Minnesota Press.

GARFINKEL, H. (1956) 'Conditions of successful degradation ceremonies'. *American Journal of Sociology*, Vol. 61, March, pp. 420–4.

HALPIN, A. (1966) *Theory and Research in Administration*. New York, Macmillan. pp. 131–249.

HOYLE, E. (1972) 'Facing the difficulties'. *Unit 13 of Course E283*. Open University.

JENKINS, D. J. (1972) 'Curriculum development and reference group theory'. *Unit 15 of Course E283*. Open University.

LORTIE, D. C. (1969) 'The balance of control and autonomy in elementary school teaching'. In ETZIONI, A. (ed.) *The Semi-Professions*. New York, Free Press. pp. 1–53.

MERTON, R. K. (1968) *Social Theory and Social Structure*. New York, Free Press. pp. 185–214.

MUSGROVE, F. (1973) 'Power and the integrated curriculum'. *Journal of Curriculum Studies*, Vol. 5, No. 1, pp. 3–12.

REISS, A. (1968) 'The social integration of queers and peers'. In RUBINGTON, E., and WEINBERG, M. S. (eds.) *Deviance, the Interactionist Perspective*. New York, Collier-Macmillan. pp. 371–81.

ROSTOW, W. W. (1966) *The Stages of Economic Growth*. Cambridge, Cambridge University Press.

SCHOOLS COUNCIL INTEGRATED STUDIES PROJECT (1972) *Exploration Man: An Introduction to Integrated Studies*. London, Oxford University Press.

SCHOOLS COUNCIL (1970) *Integrated Studies in the First Years of Secondary School*. Pamphlet No. 7. London, Schools Council.

SCHOOLS COUNCIL (1971) *Choosing a Curriculum for the Young School Leaver*. Working Paper No. 33. London, Evans/Methuen.

SHIPMAN, M. D. (1971) 'Innovation in schools'. In WALTON, J. (ed.) *Curriculum Organization and Design*. London, Ward Lock. pp. 11–16.

SHIPMAN, M. D. (1972) 'Contrasting views of a curriculum project'. *Journal of Curriculum Studies*, Vol. 4, No.2, pp. 145–53.

SHIPMAN, M. D. (1973) 'The impact of a curriculum project'. *Journal of Curriculum Studies*, Vol. 5, No. 2.

STURDY, J. (1972) 'The role of the publisher'. *Dialogue*, No. 12, Autumn, p. 4.

WALTON, J. (ed.) (1971) *Curriculum Organization and Design*. London, Ward Lock.

WASNEDGE, R. (1971) 'Whatever happened to Nuffield Junior Science?'. *Where*, Vol. 59, July, pp. 209–12.

Index